LIONEL TRILLING

38 - 59

ROBERT BOYERS

LIONEL TRILLING

NEGATIVE CAPABILITY AND THE WISDOM OF AVOIDANCE

A LITERARY FRONTIERS EDITION

UNIVERSITY OF MISSOURI PRESS

COLUMBIA & LONDON, 1977

Copyright © 1977 by
The Curators of the University of Missouri
Library of Congress Catalog Card Number 77–7322
Printed and bound in the United States of America
University of Missouri Press, Columbia, Missouri 65201

Library of Congress Cataloging in Publication Data

Boyers, Robert.
    Lionel Trilling : negative capability and the wisdom
of avoidance.

    (A Literary frontiers edition)
    1.   Trilling, Lionel, 1905–1975—Criticism and
interpretation.
PS3539.R56Z6   818'.5'209   77–7322
ISBN 0–8262–0228–4

To my wife Peg—
who read Trilling with me—
and for Lowell & Zachary Meyer Boyers

LIONEL TRILLING

BACK in 1924, I. A. Richards could in all candor write that "critics have as yet hardly begun to ask themselves what they are doing or under what conditions they work." Richards was quite right, of course, and it is a fact of the literary life that ever since the publication of his *Principles of Literary Criticism*, critics have done nothing so compulsively and so tediously as to ask just those questions. How strange, then, that the single critic who, in these fifty years or so, has done more than others to make of his calling an honorable and distinctive mode of literary expression should have concerned himself so little with the theory of his discipline or with the particular school affiliations of his thought. Lionel Trilling has been variously described as a liberal, a conservative, a patriarch, an aesthete, a moralist, and so on.[1] Though in his writings he consistently expressed a profound aversion to ideological thinking and was scrupulously fair and responsive to rival points of view, he came especially in his later years to be derided for various kinds of inflexibility and for downright obtuseness. Why so many literary people should have thought him vulnerable to their probings—malicious and otherwise—we cannot confidently say, but there is no doubt that a critic of his eminence was hurt in the eyes of many detractors by his seeming to operate so blithely, without benefit of theory or system. Though Trilling contradicted himself on occasion, and was of two minds on almost everything he touched, he knew what he was doing, or thought he knew. The pleasure we take in his enduring work is a pleasure

1. Philip Rieff, in *Fellow Teachers* (New York: Harper and Row, 1973), designates him "Jew of Culture."

1

in confronting a unified sensibility whose general absence our culture has persistently bemoaned through all the years of this century. Trilling didn't have to erect a system over the gaps in his thought or the cosmic vacancies in the world view he shared with his readers. He was interested in himself as he was interested in others, and had a decent respect for the job of work he was suited to perform. The mean and envious fellow who complained a few years ago that "It never occurs to [Trilling] that we may not want to know what is on his mind" inadvertently located one of Trilling's central strengths. Though Trilling doubted most things, including his own opinions, feelings, and ideas, he never seemed to have doubted his own capacity to be interesting to other persons with a similar capacity to be sincerely concerned about the art and thought of their own time, and about the cultural heritage they had been invited to look after. Because Trilling knew what he was intended to do, he had little time to ask those questions that others with a more purely "professional" stake in the career of letters had so often to ask.

Trilling was more than a critic, of course, though it is difficult to say what term better describes him. No doubt his work bears intermittent witness to the kind of concern we associate with intellectual history, or with literary journalism, or with sheer speculative commemoration; but it is perhaps most appropriate to think of Trilling as having enlarged the possibilities of literary criticism to accommodate almost any subject—provided only that it be framed to meet the terms of a focused and largely thematic enquiry. What is more, Trilling may be said to have operated as a critic even in his occasional "creative" works, those audacious fictions so often anthologized and debated that many must often have wondered why a man who lived to be seventy should not have written more. We say that he operated as a critic, without meaning any disrespect to his stories or to his one novel *The Middle of the Journey*, because he seemed always to be interested primarily in ideas and in the process of thought itself. When we think of his investment in moral issues, of his love of beautiful words and generous sentiments, we think necessarily of his decency and urbanely companionable gentleness; and we are likely then to underemphasize the strenuous, generalizing impulse in his writing so often remarked by hostile observers. For Trilling was a man bent on getting at the significance of things, and in this was perfectly willing to yield a little by way of particularity if he might thereby discover the symptomatic status of the recalcitrant object. Though Trilling was usually circumspect and prudential in his literary transactions with the world, he rarely passed up a chance to distinguish a pattern from a local detail, and openly invited the charge that he insisted too stubbornly on what he took to be the facts of life. Though he directed most of his writing to particular works of art or to artists, his abiding subject had to be reality—the hard facts and temptations of the moral life. As a critic, to be sure, Trilling thought of reality under the auspices of ideas: what men of various dispositions, experiences, and gifts thought of reality, how they made their way among the versions of the real and good and true and possible available to men in their time.

Though Trilling was interested in many ideas, in political systems as much as in Freudian theories and aesthetic programs, there were a few to which he was inexorably attracted. The object of this study is to work through the most important of those ideas in a way that will be generally helpful—especially to those who do not think that Trilling's work can stand up to careful, intermittently adversary exposition. Trilling did not often pursue an idea with the tenacity required to make it seem indisputably central in his vision. The movement of his thought was fundamentally discursive and graceful, the tone of the speaking voice uninsistent and modest. Ideas were rarely permitted to emerge as independent objects of thought whose intersection with other comparable ideas could be precisely charted or evaluated. Respecting the special rhythms and reticences of Trilling's imagination, I have nonetheless determined to lift out of the texture of his discourse the several ideas to which he returns more or less faithfully. In so lifting them, I have thought to slow down a little the easy movement of Trilling's thought, to discover just how he managed to pass from one point to another without seeming to worry very much about connections that were apt to strike some readers as tenuous indeed. What is the point at which the idea of *negative capability* needs to be joined to the idea of *will* in order for either of them to yield what Trilling thinks it should? How much did Trilling's explicit reliance on the idea of *tragedy* mask an unwillingness to acknowledge fully the presence in his thought of other ideas that more truly address his concerns? Why should an idea of *political reality* in Trilling be so helpful in getting at certain aspects of modern cultural life and so inadequate to deal with others? These are the kinds of questions posed here, questions I take to be crucial to an understanding of Trilling and of the impact he has had on our time.

Chief among the ideas to which Trilling was attracted, to judge from his published writings, was the idea of tragedy, an idea he never elaborated in any systematic way, but that he uses again and again, even in unlikely contexts. I stress his attraction to this venerable idea because it seems to me a central element in his thought, a key to the special strengths and limitations of that sensibility to which he gave so fine an utterance. He speaks of

4

the tragic, I say, even in unlikely contexts, and what could be more unlikely than the context provided by his own memorable story, "Of This Time, Of That Place"? Most readers familiar with Trilling's literary criticism will also know this story, but not all will know the brief autobiographical commentary on it he wrote for his own massive 1967 anthology of world literature entitled *The Experience of Literature*.[2] The commentary he wrote to accompany the story in 1967 is a curious and revealing document, written, he tells us, to give students some helpful notions about the possible origins of a work of literature, about the specific relation between actual experience and a particular story. In fact the commentary accomplishes much more: it indicates the kinds of questions Trilling couldn't bring himself to ask and helps define the principle of his coherence as a writer. For Trilling needed, or wished, to avoid not only questions of critical purpose and methodology; by carefully manipulating certain ideas he managed as well to draw an implicit circle around what was for him a sufficient body of material and range of thoughts that lent themselves to the kind of interpretation with which he felt most comfortable. Like other successful writers, Trilling knew what he was meant to handle, and he recalled himself to his literary mission by regularly coming back to the idea of tragedy, an idea that was for him constitutive of much that he took to be involved in a genuine experience of life and of art.

In the commentary on his story, Trilling confides that he determined "from the first" to "come as close as I could to tragedy." Why? Because he conceived the young character Tertan "to be an impressive figure, in some sense heroic," one who "therefore made the demand" to

2. *The Experience of Literature* (New York: Holt, Rinehart & Winston, 1967).

be treated with something like tragic power. The argument is deliberately limited. Trilling never claims to have achieved his original conception; neither does he say how he wishes us to read the words "in some sense heroic," which cannot under the circumstances be said to speak for themselves. We understand that a certain quality of "perverse majesty" attributed to Tertan strikes Trilling as appropriate to a figure of tragic dimension, and that any person—like Tertan—clearly possessed by an idea will stand out extravagantly in a landscape as tame as ours. We observe too that Trilling goes out of his way in the text of the story to underline his primary intention, so that part two of the story begins with the words: "The question was, At whose door must the tragedy be laid?" The question posed refers most immediately to Ibsen's *Ghosts*, the assigned text in the college classroom in which the action for part two of the story is initially set. Only later on do we come to consider the implication of the classroom discussion for the drama of Tertan and his instructor. Not that Trilling is assiduous to press upon his reader the tragic element in the story. Though some variant of the word *tragedy* appears from time to time, the tone is so often slyly ironic or mock-heroic that readers are encouraged to make of the experience what they will. Even obligatory references to fate, inevitability, pity, and the status of the classic fail to press us, as well they might had Trilling insisted upon his early conceptual thrust.

The idea of tragedy, then, is central to Trilling's project as he originally framed it for himself and as he later came to explain it to readers. Why it should seem utterly beside the point in our experience of the story is a peculiarity of the literary life we should not be quick to dismiss. It is a commonplace, of course, that writers do not always know what they are doing; that they frequently account for a project in ways that seem insupportable to their readers. It is also true that some readers will be impressed by the reasonableness of an explanation that to other equally gifted readers seems incredible. Still, we expect, we demand, as readers, that a text engage us in a way that bears some necessary relation to what we take to be authorial intention. It is my experience of Trilling's story that it engages us in just this way: that we feel throughout a perfect confidence in Trilling's capacity to achieve what he intends. What is peculiar is Trilling's stated intention outside the frame of the story that it all be subsumed under the aegis of a tragic view. For if Trilling had really wanted to create anything like a tragedy, had he been even moderately capable of carrying out so special a project, he'd no doubt have taken steps to tell his story in an entirely different way. Trilling does not press the tragic dimension in his story because he knows perfectly well, in his bones, that it is at best an ironic counterpoint to his actual intentions.

The problem, of course, extends far beyond the question of Trilling's having described the intention of his story in a misleading way. The description is, in this case, clearly indicative of Trilling's practice elsewhere, when he was not so much misleading as determined to establish a view of things that would serve his purposes as a writer and assist in the entrenchment of attitudes he took to be good for all of us. Tragedy was for Trilling an idea with a particular resonance, valuable in itself for the stern and intractable demeanor it could bring to the consideration of issues otherwise frivolously engaged. The central issues in Trilling's story are issues of sympathy and responsibility. A young man named Tertan appeals for help and for support to his college English instructor, Dr. Howe. Howe is moved by the quality of the young man's appeal, by his special devotion to literature and, as he writes in the role of faculty sponsor to membership in Quill and Scroll, "by his exceptional love of all things of the mind." He feels a certain loyalty to Tertan, as he comes to appreciate the young man's devotion to him and admiration of his calling as poet. Almost at once, though, long before the end of their first and only semester together, Howe comes with mingled shock and relief to feel that Tertan is certifiably mad; that his disordered and fantastic expression is a sign not merely of unusual literary zeal and promise but of hopeless derangement. As he can no longer reasonably hope to improve Tertan's writing or to otherwise chasten his expression, Howe gives up the boy more or less completely, though with a guilty conscience, and turns the "case" over to the college dean for official action. Clearly, he feels, the boy is beyond instruction in rhetoric or in textual analyis. His "tragedy," if you will, has to do with an element of waste and is summed up by Trilling in the commentary as "the sad irony of a passionate devotion to the intellectual life maintained by a person of deranged mind."

But in his commentary Trilling fails to discuss the fact that the structure of his story forbids our taking extended thought on the subject of that "sad irony." It is not Tertan but Howe who ultimately engages our attention, and every detail of the story supports our interest in the professor's handling of the "case" rather than in Tertan's intensely provoking presence. For this insight we have only to consult our general experience of point of view in fiction and to observe how Trilling's story is so arranged that everything we see is presented from Howe's perspective. That we are bound to puzzle over Tertan no one will deny, but we puzzle over him as much as we do because we are told so little about him. At best he is an instant in another character's intellectual life, a passing occasion for the indulgence of a sense of guilt or shame that most of us will know better than to indulge too often. Such a character cannot be said to take upon himself that burden of decisive action to which readers may respond with pity or fear or exaltation. Had Trilling thought to create in Tertan a tragic figure he would have worked a good deal harder to achieve a more intimate profile and to move the character more firmly to the center of the main action. I contend that his reason for not doing so was that he did not wish to represent Tertan's dilemma as anything but pitiable and mildly teasing. No matter the feelings Howe entertains for Tertan, or the specter of guilt that passes intermittently before him whenever he sees the boy: Trilling knows who he is, what he can handle, and Tertan is for Trilling the unmistakable, unapproachable other. Is it reasonable to say so when Trilling is not himself a character in the story? Insofar as we can tell, the authorial voice that speaks in the story is Trilling's, and the identification with Howe which had seemed certain in our reading of the story is fully confirmed by Trilling's more recent commentary. When Trilling writes of Howe's ambivalent yielding of Tertan's case to the keeping of the Dean, of Howe's fear and self-doubt, he is writing of himself, and there is no point in pretending we may not say so.

Why, then, should Trilling have spoken of tragic intention in accounting for his story, and why should the completed text contain some small warrant for our looking at it in that light? Trilling would have liked to confer tragic stature upon Howe, not upon Tertan, and though he could not quite bring himself to affirm that intention, his commentary provides whatever detail we may need to understand the calculations involved. Though the "impressive," in "some sense heroic" aspects of the young man who became the character Tertan were originally responsible for encouraging a tragic direction, Trilling came quickly to discover where he really wanted to go. "Quite without my bidding," Trilling tells us, the image of the opposing or alternate student character "popped up before me." Blackburn is in many ways a perfect foil to Tertan, but his presence in the story might seem to undercut that dimension of seriousness and severity we associate with tragic intensity. For Blackburn is a buffoon, and the problems he presents are decidedly parochial and practical in a way that nothing involving Tertan can ever be. What, after all, does Blackburn represent? He tries to manipulate his teacher, first with flattery, later by playing upon his sympathies, finally by malevolence and open threat. Though anyone might well hesitate a while before making up his mind, no teacher of my acquaintance would seriously succumb to Blackburn's wiles without severely compromising his self-respect. Though Blackburn presents Howe with a few choices, none of them can be said to be tragic. Next to Tertan, Blackburn is an obvious case. His instructor can do nothing but despise him for his failing work and grossly stupid manipulations.

But there is more in Blackburn, for Trilling, at least, who writes: "Blackburn's malevolence rescued the teacher from being merely a sensitive, sympathetic, observing consciousness. By putting Howe in some danger, it made him that much more of a person; it made him someone with a fate and required that he should not only feel but act." In other words, Blackburn's presence in the story makes it possible to cast Howe as the tragic figure, "someone with a fate" who can "not only feel but act" and thereby be judged. What is the judgment? Inevitably, that Howe behaved quite respectably where Blackburn was concerned; that he extended to the boy every advantage, despite his unavoidable distaste, and acted decisively to put an end to the boy's nonsense only when generosity had been made impossible. One finds in Howe's dealings with the boy nothing extraordinary, of course, and while there is bound to be "some danger" in almost any emotional transaction, Howe cannot really be said to have acted bravely or without thought of practical consequence in finally silencing Blackburn. Howe undertakes to perform an action, it is true, but the action is bound to seem paltry rather than tragic by comparison with his behavior towards Tertan. It is clear that Trilling wished to portray his alter ego, Dr. Howe, as a man confronted by several choices to which he was equal in his own way; as a man, moreover, for whom no action or refusal of action is likely to seem easy or certain. In this Trilling succeeds. We may not especially admire Howe or approve his particular decisions, but we are forced to respect the burden of consciousness and guilt he willingly takes upon himself. If he resolves important problems rather too simply, he continues to live with his decisions in a way that does credit to him as a man of sensitivity and of intellect. What is unsatisfactory is Trilling's attempt to claim for Howe a stature to which he is definitely not entitled. For what Trilling must have understood in composing his brilliant story he could not bring himself to acknowledge or engage in the commentary: Blackburn was not required to "rescue" Howe "from being merely a sensitive, sympathetic, observing consciousness." The reader had, after all, every reason to think him capable of betrayal, self-deception, and expediency in his treatment of Tertan. Blackburn is useful in supporting an idea of relatively minor importance, in Trilling's formulation: "that there are kinds of insanity that society does not accept and kinds of insanity that society does accept." This idea, as Trilling goes on to indicate, is too easily formulated and too explicit to serve as primary focus of a powerful story.

The idea is not, however, without a certain provocative potential, for if Trilling had wished to confer a kind of tragic stature upon Howe, he would also have had to consider the relation between tragic character and social convention. Nowhere in his commentary does he make an effort to do so. Instead, he insists quite strenuously upon a mode of judgment that, though operant in the story, had there been refined and qualified almost to the degree of attenuation. The judgment is, quite bluntly, psychiatric and dismissive: "Nothing, I fear, can reverse the diagnosis of Tertan's illness." Or, in the same mode, "no psychiatrist would fail to say that Tertan must soon go to a mental hospital." All this, apparently, by way of implicit justification of a decision made by a character in a story. No doubt Trilling had himself come in for a good deal of abuse on account of that decision, and he was candid enough to take up the challenge in immediate terms and to accept the imputed identification between Howe and himself. But what is the underlying assumption of the defense he mounts? It is that character, even in its most articulate and developed form, takes its primary shape and direction from social convention and that there are creditably sensible ways of handling what might seem at first impossible dilemmas. That we can never be entirely confident about the moral justification of our actions is a fact we cannot blink; more, if we wish to live comfortably in the world we must accept as well a measure of guilt and pain that no civilized person can fully banish.

It is surprising that Trilling should have flirted so long with the idea that he was expressing in all of this a tragic conflict. No matter what partial theory of tragedy one accepts, there is a single unquestionable truth one will necessarily credit: to its protagonist, a tragic action is extraordinary, difficult, and painful in the extreme. Tragedy is not a way of life nor a culturally approved way of solving thorny problems. It is a vision of possibility that is at odds with the easy, the approved, the sensible, and the familiar. If, as a vision of possibility, it presents to a suitably receptive person an inevitable action, the inevitability is a function of a character that is in significant ways inflexibly resistant to sensible solutions. Nothing could be further from Howe's nature, nor, to be consistent, from Trilling's. We are confronted here with what may well be termed a noble, but not a heroic character; with a character who felt no embarrassment at having learned how to cope and who could be positively scornful toward others who cultivated the romanticism of failure or grotesque extremity. Trilling's insistence upon Tertan's illness, upon the boy's having passed beyond the help of a mere pedagogue, is at once sensible and disappointing, as Trilling surely knew. It is one thing to recommend that a young man seek psychiatric help, quite another to walk away from him as though one's human obligation had been fully discharged in making the recommendation. Trilling deals with this by asserting that the young man "was on the way to being beyond the reach of ordinary human feelings." This is to say that nothing could be done for Tertan in an ordinary human way and that the "unnecessary remorse" Trilling continued to feel at his "disloyalty" was but the reflection of a tragic awareness.

The tragic awareness would, in this case, revolve about the recognition of the irremediable in our experience. As such, it would conform to classic notions of the tragic and would seem therefore to be, in its way, a sound conclusion. The difficulty is that Trilling's emotion in the commentary, Howe's in the story, is not generated by Tertan's problem, which may indeed have been "irremediable" in the long run. As the dominant recording consciousness of the story is Howe's, or Trilling's, our attention is primarily focused on the exertions of that consciousness. If the circumstance before us is tragic, it will have to involve our sense of those exertions pitted against conditions to which the recording consciousness proves equal, though it be doomed by virtue of its very strength. This we cannot say of Trilling's response to Tertan. Though Tertan may be beyond clinical recovery, he is not as a person beyond receiving an additional measure of human solicitude. Trilling's "unreasoning remorse" addresses his own failure to provide that solicitude, not Tertan's illness. Nor is the remorse excessive from what we can tell. Perhaps the words *disloyalty* or *betrayal* are too strong to indicate Trilling's failure here, for the failure is, it would seem, a failure of courage, and who is so magnificent as to be able to accuse Trilling of deficiency in so treacherous and uncertain a domain? All we can securely say is that tragic awareness is not really at issue here, that the courage to see and to press is as absent, finally, as the courage to undertake further elusive intercourse with the afflicted person. Even so staunch a Freudian as Trilling was to become, especially in his later years, would have had in the service of tragic truth to do more than consign Tertan to the perdition of the eternally hopeless. Freud would not have turned away so readily from Tertan, had the young man been his patient and shown himself resistant to a proper transference relationship. Was it not Freud, in fact, surely Trilling's intellectual hero, who taught us to be wary of normative judgments, who urged the most careful distinctions be made between "worthless persons" and "resistant patients"? Though Tertan may well have remained resistant to the kind of "therapy," literary or otherwise, Trilling might have "wasted" upon him, he was so clearly not a "worthless person" that he might well have repaid the debt incurred —in human terms at least. Had Trilling, or his character Howe, asked the basic Freudian questions, he might have achieved tragic stature by coming up against the intractability of the materials on which he would nonetheless have continued to work. Then the irremediable might have emerged into consciousness as a living fact, to be suffered, not used to justify a species of lofty withdrawal.

The critic Richard Chase wrote some twenty years ago a study of contrasts between English and American versions of reality. One part of that study, entitled "The Broken Circuit," has especially important things to say on the matter before us. The English novel, Chase remarks:

> is notable for its great practical sanity, its . . . moral centrality and equability of judgment. Oddity, distortion of personality, dislocations of normal life, recklessness of behavior, malignancy of motive—these the English novel has included. Yet the profound poetry of disorder we find in the American novel is missing, with rare exceptions . . . . Radical maladies and contradictions are reported but are seldom of the essence of form in the English novel . . . it gives the impression of absorbing all extremes . . . into a normative view of life. In doing so, it shows itself to derive from the two great influences that stand behind it—classic tragedy and Christianity [according to which] character moves through contradictions to forms of harmony, reconciliation, catharsis, and transfiguration.[3]

The distinction Chase draws has by now become almost a commonplace of our thinking on the relative forms and merits of English and American fiction, but I am more interested for the moment in what it helps us to see in Trilling. Surely, though Trilling finds a place in his writing for "the profound poetry of disorder" Chase locates in the American novel tradition, it is a poetry deliberately circumscribed, set off from the dominant vision of the whole. Tertan's harangues, his flights of momentary inspiration, his verbal seizures, do surely qualify as "poetry

3. See Richard Chase, *The American Novel and Its Tradition* (New York: Doubleday & Co., Inc., 1957).

of disorder," and move us to a kind of exotic pleasure and desire for more, and better. But they have a place, are assigned a place by an imagination at once attracted and frightened: they are mad, are quite literally intolerable. In so moving to set off Tertan's disordered utterance, to tame or defuse it, Trilling demonstrates his affinities with the tradition of the English novel, with its thrust toward an engrossing "practical sanity," its gift for "absorbing all extremes . . . into a normative view of life."

Trilling's story succeeds as well as it does because it is all of a piece; the commentary on the story misleads because it refuses to see the dimensions and limitations of sensibility that make for that kind of normative unity. Chase's account of the English tradition in the novel provides ample corrective by indicating that nineteenth-century English fiction may be said to derive from "classic tragedy and Christianity." The fact of derivation may not, of course, imply a necessary weakening of the earlier traditions, but there is a sense in which deterioration may be said to have taken place. If we recognize the tragic or Christian influence in Trilling's story, we recognize it as a faint specter, as an echo. Consider the operant terms in Chase's litany of traditional resolutions: "harmony, reconciliation, catharsis, and transfiguration." Trilling knows all too well how these terms and the ideas they convey may be said to operate in the universe we inhabit. Or, perhaps we should say, he knows and he doesn't know—knows in his story at least, where the knowledge is indistinguishable from a grasp of fictive circumstance, where he can relate to his own complicities as the foibles of character or as purposefully unregistered complexities in the delineation of consciousness. What, after all, is the "harmony" or "reconciliation" to which Trilling's protagonist figure Howe is susceptible? The final words of the story read: "She [Howe's young friend Hilda] rose on her toes and said 'Ready,' and pressed the release. 'Thank you,' she said gravely and began to dismantle her camera as he [Howe] hurried off to join the procession." The implications of Howe's "release" from further observation are too obvious to belabor, and his rush "to join the procession" must surely stand as testimony to a capacity for self-indictment which the commentary would seem to deny. Despite what he quite rightly takes to be his distinction, his difference, his sensitivity to nuance, Howe is to be caught up in that formal procession (in the story the word refers specifically to graduation ceremonies) the spirit of which is captured unforgettably in a perverse, almost iconic tableau: the Dean, symbol of all that is decent and official and resistant to unnecessary nuance, takes Howe's arm in friendly greeting and movement toward the impending ceremonial function; almost simultaneously he takes the arm of Blackburn, as the three move gravely together, the Dean "linking Howe and Blackburn." Such is the harmony or reconciliation to which the story bears witness, and to which neither Howe nor Trilling can mount anything in the way of effectual defense.

There is, to continue briefly with Chase's terms, also a debased form of "catharsis" in the story. The idea has traditionally referred, of course, to an effect produced upon the spectator of a tragic action as the result of his submission to emotions of sympathy and fear. But the release or accession of relief implied in the word *catharsis* is of a rather mundane sort as it evolves in our experience of Trilling's story. Here, a traditionally acceptable resolution is ready to hand, and no one in the story seems inordinately tempted to go against the grain of that resolution. The reader can, in the circumstances, be said to go along with the protagonist in crediting what seems the reasonable thing to do, and to be decently grateful for a way out of a troubling relation. In this sense, Howe's relief is to be our relief—hardly the formula of classic tragedy, to be sure, in which no satisfactory relief for the protagonist is conceivable or legitimately sought. Even as Howe writhes uneasily while waiting to discharge his burden in the Dean's office, "at the very moment," as Trilling concedes, "when he was rejecting the official way, he had been, without will or intention, so gladly drawn to it." The relief is further, and more permanently secured, in Howe's bemused observations on the setting of the Dean's waiting room and its capacity to settle anxious doubts: There was such a fine width of window that the white casements and walls seemed at this moment but a continuation of the snow, the snow but an extension of the casement and walls. The outdoors seemed taken in and made safe, the indoors seemed luxuriously freshened and expanded." One marvels at the lucidity of the expression even as one's pleasure is chastened by recognition of the large complicities signaled in so encompassing a domestication of the alien though bracing landscape. This is less a cathartic culmination than a species of elegant resignation. One may be forgiven for preferring Trilling's cool expressions of reticence and misgiving to the eerily clear-eyed serenity of this particular though crucial passage.

As to the final term in Chase's sequence, there is no doubt that "transfiguration" plays a part in Trilling's story. Consider, for example, the sentence, "But what Howe was chiefly aware of was that he had permitted the metamorphosis of Tertan from person to fact." Again in this sentence emphasis should properly be laid not upon Tertan but upon a development in Howe's view of himself. For Howe is distinctly affected, if not altogether transfigured, in the course of Trilling's story: he becomes a man who has made a decision which is constitutive of how he shall henceforth see himself. The story is punctu-

18

ated by such locutions as the following: "It was frequently to be with fear and never without a certainty of its
meaning in his own knowledge of himself" or "it would
always be a landmark of his life that." In classic tragedy,
of course, transfiguration has to do with a degree of recognition that convinces both viewer and actor that the vision
of irremediable necessity is terrible and unavoidable, especially for the protagonist-hero. For it is his fate, as a
function of some inflexibility of character, to be unable
to turn away from the ghastly spectacle, to be unable to
make the beneficent accommodations which so befit our
ordinary lives. Vision does not destroy Howe in Trilling's story, and we must be grateful that he manages so
well to see as much as he does without falling prey to
any encompassing hopelessness or grim fatigue. Which is
to say, we do not engage Trilling's story as we would
a tragic text. We engage it in the spirit in which it is presented. We allow ourselves to be moved, but only to a
point, in reading it, and we move gravely away from it
with some sense of having undergone a tutelary experience. If "the metamorphosis of Tertan from person to
fact" has seemed to us to have been accomplished with
rather an unbecoming promptness, we accept with Trilling that such "cases" are likely to be difficult for all of
us, whatever our courage or patience; also, that we had
sooner be moved in some general way than be focused
obsessively, like heroes of old, on some irremediable
wrong or injury. When, at the end of Trilling's story,
Howe is made to "ache" with pity, it is a pity "so general
and indiscriminate" that it cannot securely locate its object. This must be an aspect of what we have come to
call, with Trilling, the liberal imagination.

Now Trilling has had a peculiar and exemplary relation to the idea of liberal imagination. While he has set
himself up as its most authoritative spokesman, he has

very carefully set himself apart from what he takes to be its unfortunate predilections. Nowhere is the ambivalence of Trilling's position more lucidly expounded than in the essay "The Meaning of a Literary Idea," the final selection in the volume *The Liberal Imagination*.[4] This is as it should be, for though Trilling's understanding of liberal thought led him to write on a variety of subjects, he clearly took it to be a characteristic of such thought that it should engage *all* ideas as he undertook to cultivate *literary* ideas. His essay draws its strength from the persistence of Trilling's quarrel with the work of "the liberal democratic tradition," and from his ability to posit alternative modes of consciousness which, though dubious in their political implication, cannot strike a literary person as arbitrary or irrelevant. Central to Trilling's argument is the affirmation of what he calls, following Keats, "negative capability": "And this negative capability, this willingness to remain in uncertainties, mysteries, and doubts, is not, as one tendency of modern feeling would suppose, an abdication of intellectual activity. Quite to the contrary, it is precisely an aspect of their intelligence, of their seeing the full force and complexity of their subject matter." More precisely, negative capability defines itself by adopting an appropriate relation to ideas "as living things" that come into being when "contradictory emotions are made to confront each other." Thus, for Trilling, the irreducible essence of an idea is that it shall be founded upon contradiction and shall be tied to particular emotional dispositions. As such, an idea will properly recommend itself to a liberal intelligence in much the way that a work of art commands respect, appreciation, or love. "We can take pleasure in literature where

4. Trilling, "The Meaning of a Literary Idea," pp. 272–93, in *The Liberal Imagination* (Garden City, N.Y.: Anchor Books, 1953).

we do not agree," Trilling writes, "responding to the power or grace of a mind without admitting the rightness of its intention or conclusion"—but the same must be said of ideas in general, if we do not mistake the intention of all Trilling's work. When he remarks, "The pleasure I have in responding to Freud I find very difficult to distinguish from the pleasure which is involved in responding to a satisfactory work of art," he leaves little doubt of the equation he draws between general ideas and literary ideas. Notwithstanding recent dubious presumptions about the status of Freud as a great literary artist, it ought to be taken as fact that Freud and Henry James were after different things, whatever their relative merits as prose masters or as psychologists. If Freud's ideas are to be engaged with the kind of aesthetic discrimination we associate with a response to works of art, so too must the ideas of lesser writers than Freud, of political thinkers and sociologists and religionists.

There is no blinking the importance of Trilling's fundamental equation. It demands not so much "agreement," as he would say, as "intellectual assent," an assent we can grant only if we trace the plausible motive-force of the equation and its implication. This Trilling does for us, in part. There is to consider, for example, the element of pleasure. Clearly, in Trilling's terms, there is an unmistakable pleasure in the exercise of various human faculties. Insofar as we respond to ideas of varying merit with a power of aesthetic discrimination, we shall take pleasure in the use of this power and discover in the objects of our attention more than may originally have been intended in their formation. Nothing illegitimate is implied in this, for aesthetic discrimination will always involve procedures of contrast and comparison, and it is through selective juxtaposition with other objects that a particular inferior object may be made to seem interesting. Such juxtaposition may come to be, for minds like Trilling's, an intellectual habit or discipline rather than a simple strategy with obvious goals. In "Of This Time, Of That Place," Trilling moves beautifully toward an implicit juxtaposition of Ibsen's *Ghosts* and the central situation of his story as a means of testing the validity of his own idea of necessity—an idea clearly crucial to his conception of the whole. The pleasure we take in Trilling's story is a pleasure indistinguishable from the "intellectual assent" we grant ideas presented in it, even as we may stubbornly reject those ideas as practically applicable to our own lives in any perfect way. What we credit is the cogency and subtlety of the mind working through particular ideas without yielding entirely to them.

In the essay we have been discussing, Trilling also cites Eliot's famous remark on the unique distinction of James among American writers: "Henry James had a mind so fine that no idea could violate it." Trilling approves the remark, with the reservation that we do not take Eliot to have been condemning ideas in general. He was, we are assured, referring only to the abuse of ideas by the tendency of certain persons to use them to banish difficulty and terminate discussion, as though complex issues could be resolved by applying to them 'correct' ideas. In a sense we ought not to insist upon, it might be said that Trilling resorts to an idea in the unfortunate sense when, in his commentary on "Of This Time, Of That Place," he insists rather too strenuously on Tertan's madness as an indisputable fact in the face of which anyone would be helpless to act. For it is an idea of madness to which Trilling there responds, and in his treatment of that idea there is no allowance for nuance or degree, as there had been in his discussion of the same idea in such memorable essays as "Art and Neurosis" and "Freud and Literature."[5] Be that as it may, it is clear that for Trilling, as for the rest of us, there are good ideas and bad, but that what distinguishes a liberal intelligence from any other is its capacity to exercise aesthetic discrimination in adopting a relation to any given idea. Whatever James's politics, his attitudes towards Jews or ideas about the status of women, he had in the most important sense a decently liberal intelligence: he was interested in ideas as "living things" and made no effort to disabuse himself or his readers of the contradiction and feeling bound up in them —whether the ideas happened to be his own or the ideas of a not particularly lovable character.

James is, in fact, an especially suitable focus for the consideration of Trilling's view of ideas. For example, his novels raise the question of pleasure in a provocative and sometimes disturbing way. What, we may justly ask, is the status of an idea in which we take pleasure? According to Trilling's equation, any idea to which we pay extended respectful attention must be capable of yielding some of the pleasure we associate with aesthetic experience. It must be enlarging in some sense, must call upon our discriminatory powers, must put us in mind of feelings to which we bear implicit allegiance or which inspire instinctual aversion. Clearly, moreover, if we are to address confidently the merit and status of ideas, we shall need to consider their problematic relation to the truth— both as social fact and individual conviction. These are matters James was eminently qualified to examine, and we should not be surprised that Trilling himself devoted considerable attention to James's views in this area.

One of Trilling's essays on James, the long piece

5. Trilling, "Art and Neurosis," pp. 155–75, and "Freud and Literature," pp. 32–54, both in *The Liberal Imagination*.

on *The Princess Casamassima*, has long had a reputation as standing among the finest of Trilling's works.[6] In it, Trilling dwells in a conclusive way on issues to which he returned again and again in his writings. Indeed, though he went on to grapple with the issues in memorable and more thematically focused essays like "The Fate of Pleasure"—written fifteen years after the piece on *The Princess*—he never improved upon the formulations achieved in the earlier piece.[7] Probably this was so because James's novel represented for Trilling the kind of complexity and "moral realism" which he found elsewhere to have been compromised by the imperatives of literary modernism and by the politically shallow outlook of his liberal friends. More, James's novel "told us the truth in a single luminous act of creation" which made it unnecessary for once to scout about for revealing fragments and random insights which might, in the composition of a critical essay, be forced together somewhat unnaturally to make up a consistent argument. James's novel had it all, in Trilling's view, and with minor exceptions the critic was therefore enabled to train his analytic gaze exclusively upon a single object to discover the full range of ideas to which he was compelled. In the degree that these ideas were so finely involved in the representation of feeling or the delineation of character that they resisted isolation as ideas in the abstract, they were fully susceptible to Trilling's purposes. For Trilling wanted here to get close to the texture of James's thought, if not to the dense texture of his prose, and thereby to take up a related position of his own on what he called "the spiritual circumstances of our civilization." Able as he was in this

6. Trilling, "The Princess Casamassima," pp. 55–88, in *The Liberal Imagination.*

7. Trilling, "The Fate of Pleasure," pp. 57–87, in *Beyond Culture* (New York: Viking Press, 1965).

24

case to respond to character and performance and betrayal and loss, and only secondarily to ideas associated with each of these, Trilling could himself resist some of the tendency to ironic obliquity of statement and compulsive qualification that mark so much of his work. Trilling did more than appreciate James's novel; he responded to it deeply, personally. It had become for him an emblem of several truths to which he was urged continually to bear witness. And it is just this quality of bearing witness to which we will respond most strongly and gratefully in reading again Trilling's essay.

The novel itself has been frequently discussed and debated. Though it has rarely been held in such high esteem as Trilling affords it, most commentators have conceded its interest at least, and have applauded the vivid depiction of certain characters. Where negative criticism has been most assiduous to expose the novel's deficiencies, it has struck repeatedly at the quality and accuracy of James's political imagination. Nowhere else, according to James's detractors, has the impoverishment of this imagination been more apparent than in *The Princess*, where an openly political situation sits at the center of the action. Nowhere more clearly does James fail to see or to demonstrate that he sees what actually takes place in a political universe, where individual actions may be shown to have general consequences, where ideas are translated into policies and into articulated convictions. The attack on James from this point of view has been shared by writers as various as Yvor Winters[8] and Maxwell Geismar[9]: Winters demanded "a clear set of ideas" to support

8. See the essay on James in Winters, *In Defense of Reason* (Chicago: Swallow Press, 1969).

9. Geismar's attack on James in *Henry James and the Jacobites* (Boston: Houghton Mifflin Co., 1963) is notorious—but surprisingly helpful in several ways.

the moral sense in James; Geismar, specific political ideas of which the critic can approve and that are said to be implicit in the unarticulated premises of some of James's work. Nor should it be surprising that more recent positive criticism of James should dwell, though with very different emphasis, on these aspects of James's imagination. Leo Bersani, in his book on *Character and Desire in Literature*,[10] points us toward "the Jamesian effort to coerce society into becoming an arena for the performance of the passionate fictions of James's heroes." This is a point on which Trilling has much to say, and on which he is most instructive. For Trilling did not believe that it was possible to speak of politics without speaking of the desires of men, of their "passionate fictions." The sense of a thing seemed to Trilling precisely what one had to mean when one attempted to speak of the thing itself, for what would a thing be without the recording consciousness and the special predispositions that allowed that consciousness to decide what it would feed upon? Bersani talks about "the ambiguous attitude of realistic fiction toward reality," and Trilling would no doubt have agreed. But he would have gone a good deal further in stressing the necessary ambiguity in any sensible apprehension of reality; for in the domain of attitude, of affect or idea, we are bound to be interested not in self-evident objects of attention, but in problems of vision, conflicts of will, and the like. Nor would Trilling entirely have approved Bersani's reference to "the Jamesian effort to coerce society." Society did not need to be coerced to demonstrate the various things James discovered for us. It needed, in Trilling's view, like persons in the given society, to be read, to be interpreted, to be studied with an imagination capable at once of candor and affection. Though, as we have

10. The full title is apt to be unnecessarily forbidding: *A Future for Astyanax* (Boston: Little, Brown, and Co., 1976).

indicated, he was ambivalent about everything, Trilling felt he knew with some certainty what was real and what was not, and he felt in James the presence of a sensibility that knew reality as Trilling wanted all of us eventually to know it.

What, then, did James discover in the world that his critics are uncertain he actually saw, or ought to have seen, and that Trilling so enthusiastically approves? James discovered that the world is both a fearful and compelling arena, and that those who most fully recognize and feel its complex appeal may well be the most helpless of its victims. That is the most general and fundamental, as it is also the most obvious, of James's discoveries, but it was not therefore of minor interest to Trilling. Nor could it have mattered to him that critics of the novel, like F. W. Dupee, remarking on its protagonist Hyacinth Robinson, felt that more particular and local insights were also obvious: "Hyacinth travels far to learn what he could have read any day in the *Times*: that radicals are envious."[11] For Trilling it was the quality of the discovery that mattered, not the facts of life so much as the manner in which we may be said to apprehend them. In this, as in most things, Trilling's approval is emphatically reserved for complex awareness. No matter how subtle the thought entertained, it would be appreciated only inasmuch as it had sunk deeply, as it had been permitted to meet other competing thoughts or discoveries entertained with comparable seriousness. These conditions he found to be met with consummate refinement in James. The discovery of the world's fearful seductions and positive delights was in James a genuine discovery, repeated anew in book after book. It did not matter, for Trilling, that the physical contours of "society" in James should not have seemed

11. Dupee, "In the Great Grey Babylon," p. 157, in *Henry James* (New York: Sloane, 1951).

sufficiently lifelike to satisfy many gifted readers, or that a critic like Winters should have complained that a character's "intense excitement is vastly disproportionate to any actual perception that one can disentangle." For Trilling would not have understood what Winters meant by "actual perception" and would have had to remind the critic that many objects of consciousness yield themselves only to properly receptive investigators. If Winters wanted "actual perceptions," he might surely have found them in *The Princess Casamassima*, but he would have had to be looking for things that one might legitimately hope to find in such a book.

Trilling's approach to the novel is hardly disputatious, and though he usually took into full account the critical climate surrounding a text, he rarely went out of his way to score critical points by picking fights with other critics. It is unmistakable, though, that there is an implicit response to other critics running through the essay on *The Princess*. Clearly, Trilling takes the main charge against the book to be that it is deficient where it should be strongest, in concrete delineation of political reality. This charge he counters first by explaining that the novel draws with extreme accuracy an aspect of the political climate of Europe in the nineteenth century. This aspect has to do with various currents of anarchist agitation that attracted considerable attention in the 1880s. Trilling masterfully summarizes the relation between actual events and a variety of incidents reported in the novel. He indicates, by citing various political documents, that James knew very well indeed what was involved in anarchist politics and that he saw its relation to other kinds of political agitation. All of this is useful, but it is merely preliminary to a discussion of the issues in a much more impressive and helpful way. For Trilling goes on to demonstrate that James knew how to motivate, and thereby to account for, political action in a way that went far beyond a theory of envy or of resentment or of the "actual" as Winters, for one, understood it.

What made *The Princess* "an incomparable representation of the spiritual circumstances of our civilization" was James's ability to body forth in the most convincing way his special understanding of the relation between ideas, truth, and reality. In this James may be said to have furnished exactly what was needed. Trilling could not have been less bothered by the absence of a certain kind of naturalistic detail in the novel. He recognized, with James, the central issues at the heart of political reality and saw that the insistence upon a particular kind of verisimilitude and accumulation of detail masked a desire to avoid those central issues. The issues had largely to do with the subject of will, a will that had grown disorderly and implausible in its relation to the reality it was bent on appropriating to its purposes. It is a subject to which Trilling turned frequently in his essays: in the piece on Dickens's *Little Dorrit*[12] the emphasis is especially pronounced, and one finds there within the space of a few pages reference to "transcending of the personal will," "the search for the will in which shall be our peace," and, conclusively, "the negation of the social will." But it is the essay on *The Princess* that best demonstrates Trilling's handling of the concept of will and that most cogently brings it into fruitful relation with James's treatment of the intersection of ideas, truth, and reality. Though he moves about a good deal in his essay, taking up first one issue and then another, it is quite clear that Trilling saves his most urgent concerns for last. Though he could not but be moved by the fate of Hyacinth Robinson—moved indeed to make of him what few readers

12. Trilling, "Little Dorrit," pp. 50–56, in *The Opposing Self* (New York: The Viking Press, 1955).

will wish to grant—he was moved in the more urgent and immediate way by the Princess herself.

For the Princess was, in Trilling's view, the very incarnation of disordered will. As such, she posed for Trilling a manifest threat to the liberal imagination as he understood and valued it at its best. This was, we may recall, an imagination that refused to be violated by ideas—refused, that is, to be dominated by any singular conception of reality under whose auspices one could stubbornly pretend in all good conscience that no other version of the true or real might command respect. The Princess, however, may best be described as one in whom the will has come to do the work of imagination—a symptomatic figure in our culture, as the psychoanalyst Leslie H. Farber has persistently pointed out.[13] She is, in Trilling's resonant terms, "a perfect drunkard of reality," "ever drawn to look for stronger and stronger drams." What does this mean? That the Princess installs at the center of her life a will to reality which, if it achieves what it desires, will have effectually banished the meaninglessness and unreality in which she believes she has spent most of her life. Are aristocratic personages unduly sheltered? They must walk in the gutters and rub greasy elbows with the multitudes. Do aristocrats find little to occupy their time? They must "get busy." Do cultured aristocrats spend a disproportionate amount of time—by contrast with working people—looking at fine paintings and strolling in ample gardens? They must live in a hovel, sell the paintings, burn the gardens. All the while, of course, such persons must feel that they are moving ever closer to their goal and that what they abandon is of no conse-

13. See Farber's books *The Ways of the Will* (New York: Basic Books, 1965) and *Lying, Despair, Jealousy, Envy, Sex, Suicide, Drugs, and the Good Life* (New York: Basic Books, 1976) for an elaborated theory of will.

quence whatever. The Princess beautifully exemplifies this pattern: beautifully, in the sense that she remains attractive even as she betrays her own faculties of imagination and intelligence; also, in the sense that she remains throughout a credible figure despite the extravagance of her commitment.

But we had best pay close attention to Trilling's account of the Princess, for it is in that account alone that we are permitted to grasp the symptomatic status of her character and the portent she represents for our culture. We note how it is in her relation to an idea of reality that the Princess most particularly asks to be seen:

> She cannot but mistake reality, for she believes it is a thing, a position, a finality, a bedrock. She is, in short, the very embodiment of the modern will which masks itself in virtue, making itself appear harmless, the will that hates itself and finds its manifestations guilty . . . , that despises the variety and modulations of the human story and longs for an absolute humanity, which is but another way of saying a nothingness. In her alliance with Paul [Muniment] she constitutes a striking symbol of that powerful part of modern culture that exists by means of its claim to political innocence and by its false seriousness—the political awareness that is not aware, the social consciousness which hates full consciousness, the moral earnestness which is moral luxury.

We may legitimately observe at once that so ringing a denunciation is rare in Trilling's writing and that he brings it off in this case because "the moral earnestness" in his own voice is not permitted wholly to overwhelm the general sense of analytic scruple his work ordinarily conveys. The student of James's novel may not agree that the Princess is awful in just the ways Trilling suggests, or that the symptomatic status of the character had seemed nearly so unmistakable in the original reading as it now appears to be. But the student will concede, without hesitation, that the novel is made more interesting and valuable in the light that Trilling throws upon it. His approach is definitive not in the sense that it reveals with indisputable certainty James's intentions and the precise magnitude of his achievement; it is definitive as an account of the appeal a certain kind of book is apt to make to an intelligence hungry for what the book really has to give. If it offers other kinds of nourishment to less assiduous or subtle or hungry readers, it is no less Trilling's special text than the authority of his appropriation would lead us to expect.

Let us work a little to "unpack" Trilling's passage. How to account for the assertion, "She is, in short, the very embodiment of the modern will"? The words "in short" would seem to indicate that the ground for the assertion had been adequately prepared in the observation immediately preceding. What is there in the belief that reality can be securely grasped, as one grasps a thing in one's hand, that should constitute the exercise of "modern will"? It is Trilling's contention that whatever reality may be, it may not be grasped in so certain a way. If we know what is real, we know what we may not fully grasp or satisfactorily articulate. We know the difference, that is, between what may be said to be real and what is no more than an object of will. No one can tell us where the difference lies if we do not habitually imagine the difference for ourselves. How do we know that James's Princess believes reality to be "a thing," "a finality"? By the extremity of her effort to will a satisfactory relation to it. By her insensitivity to nuances of feeling which, by virtue of experience and personal trial, she should be fully able to appreciate. The Princess seeks reality in the way that she does because she has come to feel that a more tentative and imaginative approach may obscure what she so terribly wants to be perfectly clear. Is it as obvious as

Trilling wants us to believe that her apprehension of this reality is mistaken? The exercise not of will but of imagination would provide ample correction. Suppose, for the moment, that reality seemed plausibly embodied in the aspirations of the working class; further, that one's situation afforded some temporary intercourse with living representatives of this class. The will might well counsel a reading of one's experience to consort with the predisposition to believe that one had at last confronted reality. In these terms, reality might be said to reside in the desire of particular disadvantaged persons to find themselves a place in the sun; or in their bitterness towards others who had deliberately kept them from that place; or in their inability to say just what it was they wanted beyond better food, better housing—more and more material improvements. But imagination could not be satisfied with a reading of this sort. It would need to ask questions: Are disadvantaged persons likely to be happy with a place in the sun and with the material objects they crave? Do such persons actually know what they want? Can I judge the intensity and seriousness of their desires by judging the origins and satisfactions of my own? These are questions for which no definitive answers are likely to be thought available, and it is a fact of imagination that it is always pressing itself to envision the hypothetical future and recapture the incoherent past with no valid hope of shutting off the flow of questions. Trilling's point is that fixed ideas of reality, positions, are bound to violate our sense of the elusive experience we seek; finally, that we have nothing but imagination—which is an aspect of intelligence—to help us along.

So the Princess, as "the very embodiment of the modern will," seeks to go against the grain of what is hers to know; pretends to be nothing but the agent of a general or collective urging taking shape around her to which she attaches the name "reality"; denies, finally, her own utterly willful and personal reading of affairs by yielding to an idea that she takes for life itself. In Trilling's terms, she becomes the incarnate expression of a will "which masks itself in virtue" because it "hates itself," and thus cannot bear the variety and contradiction and resolute imperfection of ordinary life. Perhaps this is not as difficult as it sometimes seems to be. Surely we know in a general way what Trilling is after in the passage. And yet, I do not think we can be too careful in making our way through the argument. In what sense, after all, may we legitimately accuse the Princess of masking herself "in virtue"? It is well to recall that Trilling speaks of an activity of will, not of the Princess herself. I do not know that it is reasonable to separate them in that way, but it may be helpful to do so. For it is an element of the activity of will that it should most often be hidden from the conscious recognition of the agent. Though the Princess wishes to participate in a revolution on behalf of a new order, she may not be described as hypocritically laying claim to a virtue that, in any case, no reader would willingly grant her. Though she does not like to hear herself described as an adventurer out for the thrill of new sensations, there is a sense in which she yields—more than a little—to the charge. If the will "masks itself in virtue," it directs its deception not at other persons but at the self. The Princess is a peculiarly modern representative of the disordered will because, lacking any prospect of divine absolution, she denies her guilt and willfully seeks to make herself believe she can be saved by doing what is not authentically hers to do.

For Trilling, we see, there is an implicit correlation between reality and truth. We cannot make contact with reality unless we have first made contact with the truth of our own nature. If we will to do what we have told ourselves to do, without having been chosen—compelled—by everything we are and have been, we shall find ourselves moving progressively further from reality as it is ours to know it. The Princess might have discovered the truth of her nature by imaginatively consulting her experience, by bringing to bear on her future prospects the full sum of her memories, wishes, and disappointments. This she fails to do because she does not wish to confront the central fact of her experience: the fact of rapacious consumption on a grand scale. To confront that fact would necessarily have proposed to the Princess the prospect of further consumption—the thought that any relation she might wish to cultivate would inevitably entail the kind of consumption to which she was drawn, and which she could not but despise. The Princess's elderly companion, Mme. Grandoni, knows very well that the lady will devour and destroy the impressionable persons with whom she chooses to conspire against 'society', and it is only by an extravagant effort of will that the Princess refuses to acknowledge as much herself. By denying the direction of her most cultivated and unshakable instincts, the foundation of her sense of pleasure, the Princess has no recourse but to go at reality armed with nothing but will. That she violates reality—does actual injury to living persons she cannot have intended to harm—is tantamount to saying that she violates as well the truth: the truth of her individual being, the more general truth Trilling identifies as "the human story."

In the concluding lines of our passage, Trilling refers yet more pointedly to the symbolic stature of the Princess as a cultural and political phenomenon. There is, he argues, a "powerful part of modern culture that exists by means of its claim to political innocence and by its false seriousness." Trilling wrote often enough on the subject of this "claim to political innocence" to make us certain that the passage takes aim at the liberal fellow-traveling he knew so well in his youth and came more and more to generalize as he grew older. In his 1947 novel *The Middle of the Journey*, Trilling described the political dimension of fellow-traveling as a condition in which it was possible both to see oneself as a radical and to stand back from the sphere of immediate political activity. This was a condition to which many middle-class American intellectuals aspired, especially during the thirties. A widely credited view of political reality had it that political life necessarily had its actors and its "sympathizers." Radical credentials could be acceptably maintained if one managed to express one's sympathies in an intermittently effectual way—by signing petitions, appearing at political rallies, providing financial assistance to radical activists in need of support, and so on. Such fellow-traveling came to be notorious for the margin of hypocrisy it tolerated and, finally, encouraged. Though this is not the occasion for examination of Trilling's novel, it may be recommended unequivocally as a study of liberal conscience assuaging its various guilts by discovering substitutes for action and for genuine engagement with conditions it wished to address. The "claim to political innocence" of which Trilling speaks in his essay is a claim to which many are drawn in the novel. It involves, more particularly, the holding of various convictions or ideas without any corresponding impulse to test their validity or their actual relation to one's own situation. As such, the "claim to political innocence" could entail a demand for revolutionary change in American society and a simultaneous refusal to be judged for complicity in abortive activities that led, shall we say, to the taking of innocent lives. Correct sentiments—solidarity with striking workers, generous attitudes towards blacks, beliefs in academic freedom, and so on—would protect liberal intellectuals from dirtying their hands and from seriously considering the consequences of their self-congratulating sympathies.

Trilling's case against "false seriousness," then, though it has a decidedly political cast, cuts in a great many directions. In the essay on *The Princess* it is interesting that he should argue the lady's "claim to political innocence" as if he were speaking of the liberal intellectuals whose shabby hypocrisies he treats in *The Middle of the Journey*. For the Princess is hardly a liberal intellectual, and inasmuch as she is grand and beautiful, we cannot but quality the contempt she arouses with a good deal of appreciation. Now Trilling never actually equates the Princess with the class of liberal intellectuals; he describes her, "in her alliance with Paul [Muniment]," as a "symbol," which is quite another thing. More, since Trilling does not in the essay refer specifically to liberals but to "that powerful part of modern culture," he may be said to refer not only to a particular class but to the disproportionate influence wielded by that class on all sorts of persons—not in American or British society alone, but in Western culture generally. This is to say that Trilling in the essay determined to generalize a specific political phenomenon which had been designated by the term *fellow-traveling*. The "claim to political innocence" referred to a more general kind of bad faith, in which one undertook to effect changes in the world without considering one's own necessary relation to those changes or to the conditions they were intended to mitigate. In attacking what he took to be a false innocence typically upheld by a "false seriousness," Trilling found himself to be moving towards a general criticism of ideas: not of individual or vicious ideas so much as ideas held in a spiritually weak or "false" way. In this, the skepticism with which he came to regard political radicalism was but an element of his more encompassing disdain for spiritually dubious adventures undertaken outside the shadow of categorical imperatives that would have bound men to their espousals and actions in a truly serious way. James's skepticism was clearly of a piece with Trilling's, and the portrait of the Princess, whatever its tenderness and delight, was unmistakably a criticism of ideas in precisely the sense Trilling took it to be. If James could not have foreseen the growth of a popular view of the world in which "false seriousness" would come to play a crucial role, he nonetheless understood perfectly the difference between a genuine and a specious idea.

We stated earlier that it was James's special contribution in *The Princess* to have properly identified and made manifest the relation between ideas, truth, and reality. Trilling's function was to sharpen the distinctions and to bring the issues into further relation with other conceptual perspectives, such as those furnished in his treatment of will and of aesthetic discrimination. It was the related conceptual perspectives that prompted Trilling to conclude his famous essay with consideration of the Princess herself. In the exemplary antagonism she presented to Trilling's ideal conception of liberal imagination at its best, she demanded not merely to be noticed, but stressed. But if Trilling took James to be saying something ultimately very discouraging about the operation of will in our time and about its unfortunate relation to ideas and to our apprehension of truth and reality, he also saw in the novel a way of handling our present difficulties. Granted, ideas had in the currency of popular and political discourse been debased to the level of ideology, in the words of the Marxist thinker T. W. Adorno, to the level therefore of "untruth, false consciousness, lie"; that ideas could not therefore be supposed to generate ever new and subtle apprehensions of the relations between things, or between feelings, or the powerful impressions produced by feelings. Ideas had become a means of abstracting what one might usefully think or espouse from anything one actually felt or had a right to claim for oneself. Granted, too, that as we had come to use ideas, illegitimately, to keep ourselves from having to acknowledge truth—especially the primary truth of our own nature—we had come progressively to lose contact with that portion of reality each is given to know. But there was yet a power that, in alliance with the faculty of imagination, might bring us out of our situation. This Trilling calls the power of love.

There is nothing quaint in Trilling's suggestion. Indeed, in its application to *The Princess Casamassima* it has sufficient resonance as almost to found a comprehensive aesthetic.[14] Briefly, the suggestion devolves upon a single observation: "The novelist can tell the truth about Paul and the Princess only if, while he represents them in their ambiguity and error, he also allows them to exist in their pride and beauty." The novel's "power to tell the truth arises from its power of love." Trilling does not mean to say that James must love all of his characters equally, or that his appreciation of the Princess's demeanor must somehow be equal to his expressed or implied disapproval of her behavior. He means actually to say something much simpler: that James was required to see each character as he was and to permit each character to develop or not as his posited personal attributes would have dictated under given circumstances. To have insisted that a character be nothing but willful, that he inspire nothing but revulsion, would have been to manage character unfairly and to per-

14. The English critic John Bayley, perhaps following Trilling's lead, formulates such an aesthetic brilliantly in a book entitled *The Characters of Love* (London: Constable, 1960) and demonstrates its uses in another more recent book, *The Uses of Division* (New York: Viking Press, 1976).

mit readers to come to terms with it too easily. It would have been, in Trilling's terms, to show a patent disrespect for the particular character as he was, to fail in the obligation of love—which is but another term for the respect we owe to individual differences in our dealings with others.

Trilling does not argue, as other critics do, that the power of love is invariably present in every successful work of creative imagination. He indicates, more modestly, that the kind of moral realism to which he is attracted, and which James exemplifies, is hard put to accomplish its ends without that power. It is a power he discovered in a wide range of characters and books and which distinguished work by writers who, in Trilling's view, made little claim to creative genius—writers like William Dean Howells and George Orwell, to whom Trilling devoted memorable essays in *The Opposing Self*. But it is in its application to general experience rather than to specific books or authors that I am most interested in this notion of power. For Trilling, we shall recall, there is an equation between literary ideas and ideas of a more general nature. It is not surprising, then, that Trilling should have concluded his essay on James with these words: "together with the imagination of disaster he had what the imagination of disaster often destroys and in our time is daily destroying, the imagination of love." Trilling would not have adopted so somber a tone for his declaration had he intended only to lament the failure of novelists to produce a certain kind of fiction. He was speaking of the steady erosion of an aspect of imagination that had a great deal to do with the achievement of moral realism. This achievement he identified only in part with a particular literary tradition; more important was its relation to the life of the liberal intelligence in general. For Trilling took it as fact that liberal intelligence was the last line of defense against an encroaching political barbarism and cultural philistinism to which many of his professional colleagues had blithely opened their arms.[15] If liberal intelligence was a function of the exercise of the power of love, the indispensable tool or instrumentality had to be the faculty of aesthetic discrimination earlier introduced.

In *The Princess* James had shown that it was possible to present characters "in their pride and beauty" while telling about them several unpleasant truths so vividly impressed that we cannot but summon the unpleasantness when, in retrospect, we try to summon the characters. Trilling thought of James's achievement in this regard as a triumph of aesthetic discrimination. Moral realism was the outcome of this exercise of liberal imagination, but it was not suitable to describe James's achievement as a moral triumph pure and simple. To do so might have been to suggest a procedure wherein James, knowing just what he felt on every character and issue before him, set about to promulgate his views by staking out identifiable moral positions. The reader may imagine how little such a procedure would have allowed for the display of that "majestically equivocal consciousness"[16] recommended to us by Trilling. Now equivocation is not in itself always a seemly option, but the element of majesty is bound to make an "equivocal consciousness" seem more than a species of mincing evasion. The quality of majesty attributed to James is a quality in certain ways indistinguishable from authority, the demeanor of command, and it is not beside the point that Trilling, in his essay, describes

15. Philip Rieff describes the contemporary "treason of the clerks" in *The Triumph of the Therapeutic* (New York: Harper & Row, 1965) and in *Fellow Teachers*.

16. The expression is taken from Bayley's *The Uses of Division* and refers there to James's novella *The Aspern Papers*.

James's special powers by asking us to "imagine a father of many children who truly loves them all," but who is no less able for all his love "to see their faults." The description goes on: "The discriminations and modifications of such a man would be enormous, yet the moral realism they would constitute would not arise from an analytical intelligence [implying a "cool dissection"] as we usually conceive it." The father, then, in Trilling's analogue, sees what his children are and sees in what ways they differ from each other and from the ideals he has imagined for them. But though he sees their errors, he is not compelled to judge them in the way that the word *judgment* often implies: in the spirit of "cool dissection" and dismissive rebuke. Which is to say, though it is a prerogative of fathers to exercise authority, to pass judgments, to be—in the quite literal sense of the word— "imposing," James's authority consists in the imperturbable cultivation of an "equivocal consciousness" whose singular business it is to see. What this indicates about the capacity for aesthetic discrimination we must examine.

Earlier we cited Trilling's contention that "we can take pleasure in literature where we do not agree, responding to the power or grace of a mind without admitting the rightness of its intention or conclusion." The capacity for this kind of pleasure is indistinguishable from the capacity to make aesthetic discriminations. But the kind of intellectual activity we describe in this way is frequently confused with another sort of intellectual activity that we may call, for the sake of convenience, artistic thinking— the consciousness of artists. The philosopher R. G. Collingwood, in his book on *The Principles of Art*,[17] has much to say on the subject of this confusion. He says,

17. Collingwood, *The Principles of Art* (New York: Oxford University Press, 1938); Oxford Galaxy ed., 1972.

for example, that though "Art is not indifferent to truth," its business is not so much to argue on behalf of any truth as to expound. The literary artist conveys a kind of truth by "thinking in a certain way and then expressing how it feels to think in that way." He knows, better than he knows anything else, his own feelings. But he also knows the world—knows it, that is, as he alone is permitted to know it, so that we can say, "The two knowledges are to him one knowledge, because these sights and sounds ["which together make up his total imaginative experience" of the world] are to him steeped in the emotion with which he contemplates them: they are the language in which that emotion utters itself to his consciousness." Nor should Collingwood's emphasis on emotion suggest the view that the artist may not have ideas. If he has them, though, he will have them not by virtue of having built them up or criticized alternate views. He simply "finds himself equipped, as it were, with certain ideas"—rather than others—"and expresses the way in which it feels to possess them." That this account of artistic thinking, and of literary art, differs significantly from any account of aesthetic discrimination we might wish to draw is unmistakable. We do not have to accept Collingwood's definitions with anything like full conviction to concede, in his terms, that artistic thinking typically pursues "not a truth of relation" but "a truth of individual fact." Critical thinking, with its powers of aesthetic discrimination, will go on to ask questions that permit us to generalize and to relate "a truth of individual fact" to other comparable facts.

James, like Trilling, was both artist and critic, a fact that is more than facile observation. Everything they wrote betrays an impulse both to expound and to generalize, to evoke and to relate. Though we think of Trilling, more than of James, primarily as a critic, we think of him also as having resisted the sort of building up of argument that is familiarly negligent about the "truth of individual fact." James, on the other hand, who was only secondarily a critic—though his critical writings have been highly influential—wrote a kind of fiction that invests heavily in the life of ideas, in the prospect of discovering or building up a view of experience by working through other views that we must learn to discard. If this were not so, Trilling could not have found in James the sustenance he sought. The fact that Trilling in his criticism, James in his fiction, managed to combine expressive functions ordinarily associated with the one mode or the other is not without a very peculiar interest. In itself, the fact does not guarantee for James's novels or for Trilling's essays a literary stature they had each to earn in a variety of other ways. But the fact does in part account for a quality of sensibility the two men had in common, for all their differences of temperament and conviction. For both Trilling and James had a very large endowment of negative capability. This is properly identified as an achievement of sensibility, not an ideological stance. The endowment was such, in both cases, that Collingwood's distinction between artistic thinking and critical or philosophical thinking fails to find adequate support in our evaluation of their work. Indeed, Collingwood recognized that the distinction, for all its cautionary power, might well fail to hold up: "In the limiting case where each [form of thought or writing] was as good as it ought to be, the distinction would disappear." The negative capability we take to inform both Trilling and James at their best is a function of an uneasy relation both to individual fact and to the cultivation of abstract ideas. No one knows for certain how either writer came to acquire negative capability, but in general it may be said to issue from the same region of experience that produces taste. There is, of course, as

Matthew Arnold often observed, a taste in intellectual matters as there is in the ordinary objects we consume. There is as well, as Arnold similarly noted, a conscience in the selection of ideas and in the response to works of art. Negative capability, as an endowment of sensibility, clearly expresses a taste in ideas and an implicit principle of selection among kinds of feeling. As the author of a book on Arnold, Trilling was fully equipped to appreciate the operation of such an endowment in others, like James, and to cultivate the gift in himself. He understood, as few of us have been able to understand, that the fact of individual feeling has an intrinsic value no judgment can gainsay but that it threatens always to overwhelm the capacity for judgment in a way we must resist if we are not to be denied rarer or finer feelings we may not yet have learned to experience. Insofar as individual objects of experience are "steeped in the emotions" with which we "contemplate" them—Collingwood's terms again— we may be well advised to cultivate an alternative capacity for disinterested contemplation so that comparison or relation may chasten the extremity of our involvement.

Is this what Keats meant by negative capability? When he warned against an "irritable reaching after fact and reason," did he intend thereby to impugn some aspect of our loyalty to feeling, to recommend a capacity of reservation in our transactions with emotionally imposing facts, objects, or ideas? Trilling's famous essay on Keats[18] is endlessly instructive on the question of Keats's original intention. Though I do not wish to pursue the argument in detail, there are a few points we must note. (1) Trilling cites an important passage from a letter of Keats, in which the poet says, "The only means of strengthening one's intellect is to make up one's mind about nothing—to let

18. Trilling, "The Poet as Hero: Keats in His Letters," pp. 3–49, in *The Opposing Self.*

45

the mind be a thoroughfare for all thoughts." Trilling finds the passage "questionable" and remarks that "Exclusion is quite as much a part of the intellectual process as inclusion, and making up one's mind is not only the end of intellection but one of the means of intellection." (2) Trilling wishes to defend Keats against his detractors, despite what he takes to be obscurities in the notion of negative capability. To defend Keats, he tells us, we must "have in mind the kind of person" to whom Keats originally addressed his thought, and to whom it will always be fully relevant. This is a person "far too doctrinaire in his intellect" and subject to an "oversystematic process of thought"; also, a person who, in Keats's words, "will never come at a truth so long as he lives; because he is always trying at it"—a person, therefore, incapable of "remaining content with half-knowledge." No less a thinker than Coleridge was subject to this description, in Keats's view. (3) Trilling finds especial merit in Keats's view of negative capability as making possible "the poetic vision of life." This is a vision of truth, glimpsed under the auspices of beauty, which is available only to a self that, in Trilling's words, "is certain of its existence, of its identity," which does not, therefore, require "the armor of systematic certainties." (4) The capacity for tragic awareness is dependent, at least in part, on negative capability: "To remain content with half-knowledge," says Trilling, "is to remain content with contradictory knowledges; it is to believe that 'sorrow is wisdom' and also that 'wisdom is folly.' " Tragic knowledge is, for Trilling, an exalted form of wisdom and is founded on painful awareness of irremediable contradiction in the fabric of life. To abide the given in a spirit of tragic determination is to imagine the possibility of "ugly or painful truth seen as beauty."

It is not at all decided, then, that Keats originally intended to recommend precisely the species of reservation we find in the work of Trilling and James. But he would surely have approved the irony they direct at ideas presented apart from the desires they express, or disguise. If Keats's sensibility was luxurious and openly sensual in a way that neither James's nor Trilling's was, he would yet have admired in them the operation of an aesthetic discrimination that inclined them to resist an "over-systematic process of thought" and to cherish the spectacle of tragic contradiction. But Keat's understanding of negative capability, in the version Trilling gives of it, is more particularly useful to our reading of Trilling's thought than we may yet have imagined. It provides, in fact, an indispensable basis for consideration of the essay on James, which I've not forgotten, and one vital aspect of which we have yet to examine. That the reader may see at once the inevitable connection here, we immediately call attention to the character of James's protagonist, Hyacinth Robinson; to James's representation of him as a person who does not make up his mind about anything; to Hyacinth's persisting resistance to the doctrinaire certitudes of his friends; to the character's distinction of "remaining content with half-knowledge"; to his troubling lack of confidence in his identity or the viability of his continued existence—despite what seems in every other way to be a magnificent endowment of negative capability; and finally, to Trilling's description of Hyacinth as a genuine tragic figure, "a hero of civilization." The reader will recognize in this inventory of crucial elements a persisting reference to the theory and defense of negative capability which is not a matter of contrivance but of necessity. Trilling saw himself as standing somewhere between figures like Keats and James. He took them into himself and made their ideas and ways of looking at the world his own. His applauding James for an achievement of negative capability indicated quite plausibly that we should find the key to the one in the precinct of the other. It is no less certain that Trilling is himself to be discovered there, at the point where negative capability ceases to be entirely theory or caution and becomes instead the index to a life.

Hyacinth Robinson is that life. As a character in a particular work of fiction, he is interesting but not as compelling as we might expect if we were judging only from the large interest other characters take in him. What is decisive for the attention he does compel is the growth we observe in his character. Hyacinth is subject in James's novel to a kind of enlargement of faculties that few persons in actual life may be said to undergo. Since *The Princess Casamassima* is a long novel, the process of growth is permitted to evolve slowly, and readers are permitted to single out stages in the process which, again, are rarely discernible in the flux of ordinary life. Also worth remarking is James's evident concern to provide a basis for this growth, to establish the character—with respect to genetic background, educational opportunity, rooted personal attributes, and so on—in such a way that his progress is at once credible and powerfully affecting. The success of the portrait owes much to the loving detail in which the character is drawn, but it may owe even more to James's insistence upon bringing the figure into tentative relation with other characters whose impact Hyacinth must feel and record without allowing them to compromise the developing thrust of his nature. To manage such a portrait required infinite tact, and James was surely equal to the task. Though it is not certain that James saw the task as Trilling saw it in his essay, he surely would have gone a good part of the way with Trilling in crediting Hyacinth's growth as a superb achievement in the context of those general penalties exacted by civilization from each of us in greater or lesser degree.

Hyacinth's growth is, in many respects, an elusive thing. Trilling says of him at one point, "It is as a child that Hyacinth dies; that is, he dies of the withdrawal of love." To say this is to identify the quality of Hyacinth's growth as a very limited, though fully impressive, thing: if Hyacinth remains in crucial respects a child; if he acquiesces in a condition—partly imposed by his diminutive size—wherein, as Trilling describes it, he is "detached from the sexual possibility and disclaims it"; if, finally, he looks to other adults for a reason to carry on with his own difficult life—we may justly say that he grows more as a symbolic presence than as a living person. In fact, Hyacinth comes to think of himself more as a symbolic figure than as anything else. Trilling's reading finds its authority in James's original depiction of the character. A living person generally grows in a variety of ways that are not separable. Though we do speak of "intellectual growth" or "emotional growth," or of the prospects of the one without the other, in living persons there are ordinarily correspondences that befit our thinking in terms of organic wholes. Such correspondences are also "normative" in realistic fiction, and we have already cited Trilling's attempt to claim for *The Princess* a "realistic" foundation in the political events of the 1880s. With Hyacinth, though, we are on rather different ground. He grows—not intellectually merely, but as a person capable of fine renunciations, of carefully modulated feelings. Yet he remains, somehow, a child, a child who compels more than pity, who compels no less a critic than Trilling to consider him the very type of the modern tragic hero. Though I can hardly go along with Trilling there, any more than I could credit his comparable "reading" of his own story and of Dr. Howe, I should think we have much to learn from Trilling's theory of *The Princess*. For if Hyacinth may be said to grow in an impressive way, and yet to remain a child, he must grow as a symbolic presence: as one who comes to think his thoughts, feelings, decisions important not because they express him but because they represent something the world may not be ready to appreciate. There is nothing "wrong" with such a conviction except insofar as it may be said to nurture delusional fancies that might otherwise remain unthinkable. To think oneself a symbolic presence may not necessarily imply other leaps of thought, but surely a possible consequence would be a conviction that one's actual life was paltry next to one's representative status. Or the conviction that symbolic presences are not permitted to actualize themselves as real persons without thereby compromising their significance. I think it is fair to say that Hyacinth falls prey to such convictions and that Trilling, for all the acuteness of his "reading," fails to see why, for Hyacinth, there was no other way. Could it be that, as something of a symbolic presence himself, though in no way "childish" or "inactual," Trilling was unable to think past the function of the symbol to its underlying sources and potential consequences? We shall have to see.

In James's novel, Hyacinth's growth is presented as only partly inevitable. There is a sense in which he had to grow—such were the conflicts deposited in his nature by the circumstances of his birth and the peculiarities of childhood upbringing. There is even a sense in which the character may be said to be 'impoverished' along lines indicated by Bersani in his discussion of obsessively psychological fictions[19]: "Everything which characters say and do now can be traced back to a determining structure from the past which impoverishes present behavior by making it both tautological and excessively coherent." Despite the coherence in the portrait and our sense

19. Leo Bersani, *A Future for Astyanax*; see especially the chapter, "Realism and the Fear of Desire."

throughout that we know and remember what Hyacinth "comes from," we cannot help admiring him—at least a little. "Impoverished" his behavior may well be, but we judge him by a norm of mature psychological comportment which does not usually do justice to the finer features of a "presence" whose major achievements are aspects of pure vision and sensibility. James's portrait refuses to be "merely" psychological; he insists that there are qualities in Hyacinth that we do not know how to explain or, finally, to evaluate. Trilling sees these qualities as visionary, even compares Hyacinth to Yeats for the complexity of his awareness. We know that vision has to come from some place, some experience we've been able to make use of in more than a practical way. Hyacinth's gifts suit him to make especially good use of his experiences with the Princess herself and with the world she —more decisively than anyone else—opens up to him.

It is as a result of these experiences that Hyacinth attains what we have called negative capability. Though the words declare a distinction that is in part a matter of temperament or of innate sensibility, they also describe an active experience of achieved mastery. Trilling writes that "By the time Hyacinth's story draws to its end, his mind is in a perfect equilibrium," that his awareness of "social horror" is balanced by "his newer sense of the glory of the world." This balanced sensitivity, this ability to exist—albeit provisionally and temporarily—with no "irritable reaching" for resolution of the conflict by which one is bound, is what we mean by negative capability. Hyacinth does not need to decide which is more true— his one "sense" or the other. He knows that each is true and cannot be fully reconciled with the other. He knows there are no "ideas" which will solve the problem, insofar as it is a problem. Ideas too are for him provisional means of addressing a condition of being—his own—which is a function of unusually heightened awareness. This too is a feature of negative capability: if the words are to declare a distinction, they must refer to an equilibrium maintained with difficulty, an awareness that is keyed to powerful appreciations, not to the mild depression of a habitual resignation. Trilling loves Hyacinth because the character suffers manfully in the service of an ideal that has no practical issue—because he cultivates an appreciation of beautiful things without intending to use them or to rely on them for a new sense of his own self-importance.

But what is it, yet more precisely, that Hyacinth achieves? His friendship with the Princess introduces him to the presence in the world of a kind of beauty that seems to take no notice of itself or to ask the approval of others. He responds to this beauty first in the person of the Princess herself; later, in the fittings and spaces of her estate at Medley; finally, in the treasures of European art to which he is exposed on his trip to the Continent. Hyacinth had been earlier depicted as unusually susceptible to the elegances of form, demonstrating a susceptibility remarkable in one so little accustomed as he to the advantages of aesthetic education. But he had never shown how far he might be influenced, for good or ill, given repeated contact with the cultural inheritance of his civilization. And no doubt he should not have been so impressionable as he came to be had it not been for the period of his extended intercourse with the Princess, the opportunity given him to live—more than to visit—at Medley, to feel if only temporarily as though the great treasures might well have belonged to him. The opportunity, as it were, to participate in the life of beautiful things, to savor an intimacy with them more fancied than realized, has to be taken as decisive in Hyacinth's developing experience of himself and his fate. Though Trilling is hard on the Princess, as we earlier indicated, he does not hesitate to acknowledge the centrality of her influence in bringing Hyacinth to the presence we admire. What Trilling does not sufficiently appreciate, I believe, is the specific failure of vision that accompanies Hyacinth's growth.

The mind "in a perfect equilibrium" has got to be a peculiar instrument. It must register experiences of widely varying nature and novelty as though, in a sense, it had been prepared for anything. It must, that is to say, accept experience in the spirit of active resignation: it must not succumb merely, but must work to adjust and locate sensations in accordance with the requirements of an equilibrium that is bound—in living persons—to be unstable. Though every mind will work in this way to some degree, a mind like Hyacinth's—"in a perfect equilibrium"—will no doubt register the imperative of fine balances in a striking way, will cultivate the vision of resemblance and distinction compulsively. It will discriminate, if we may put it so, "like mad." And it will make its discriminations chiefly by applying to everything a range of normative criteria that it has learned to cherish, to uphold as though there were no other. Whether or not one considers this application of normative criteria a serious limitation or failure of vision will depend on the valuation placed on the criteria themselves. Trilling clearly thought Hyacinth had chosen well—too well, in fact, for his own good. Hyacinth is, of course, condemned to death by his choice, and though Trilling thinks this a great pity, he thinks also that it could not be helped, and that we had best under the circumstances take heart at this spectacle of a tragic demise. But what, we ask again, did Hyacinth actually come to see? In what did his achievement consist? He came, or so at least Trilling's argument would have it, to demonstrate negative capability in a way that few persons can ever have known it. Trilling does not say this himself, but the view is implicit in his argument from beginning to end. Had he been willing to articulate the insight more explicitly, he'd have noted the direction in which his argument ought then to have tended. For Hyacinth's is a very special instance of negative capability. It extends to the conduct of every aspect of life in a way that Keats, for one, could not have foreseen. What would Keats have made of the scene in which Hyacinth stands out with the Prince in the darkened, drizzly streets and watches the Princess moving to and fro in her affair with Paul Muniment? What would he have made of Hyacinth's inability to do anything but watch, to register without permitting himself to desire, to wonder without accompanying penetrative thrust? This, surely, was not what the poet had in mind when he wrote of negative capability. We are not therefore mistaken to apply the words, only we had best do so with no uncertain sense of their final implication when taken past the limit of their original intention. Though Keats might well have wished to make his theory serve a whole range of ordinary human experiences, it had to be clear to him that it did not, that it referred most pointedly to those experiences that involved or invited a response closer to appreciation than to explicit avowal. Not every human experience appeals to our better sense in that way, and we abuse our gifts and violate our relations with others if we insist on appreciation when it should be quite obvious that it will not do. Trilling celebrates Hyacinth's ability to relate to other persons and to every option before him in the spirit of the passionately disinterested connoisseur who is too good to be violated by a practical idea of what had best be done. It is the impulse to celebrate Hyacinth in these terms which permits Trilling to speak of "the proper condition for the spirit of man" without taking sufficient thought of the abuses to which his position commits him.

We cannot fail to see that Trilling has a position in all of this, that it is at once an aesthetic and a political position. Trilling was himself the first to recognize that intellectuals often mistake their insights for objective judgments and refuse to acknowledge what they are doing and what they hope to gain. By his approval of Hyacinth, though, by his extension of the ideal of negative capability to many figures who might ultimately have been examined in other ways, Trilling indicated he was not always resistant to unfortunate predilections. Trilling did not trace with anything approaching candor what he took to be the likely consequences of the positions he came to take. He allowed himself a large margin of sheer sentiment in the face of issues he could not hope to address—to his own satisfaction—by taking a position. Though he knew better than to stake out unduly large claims for sheer aesthetic consciousness and the discriminations it enabled, he granted privileged status to a dubious practice described by Saul Bellow's character Mr. Sammler as "aesthetic consumption of the environment." Bellow's novel works out the consequences of this practice in a way that Trilling does not permit himself to do.

The criticism of Trilling pursued here was begun twenty years ago by Joseph Frank.[20] In "Lionel Trilling and the Conservative Imagination" Frank noted that "the pervasive disillusionment with politics [observed by so many intellectuals in the fifties] was given its most sensitive, subtle, and judiciously circumspect expression in the criticism of Lionel Trilling." Not that Trilling set out to put politics aside, or to pretend that the important political issues had been decided. What his work accom-

20. See Frank, *The Widening Gyre* (New Brunswick, N.J.: Rutgers, 1963).

plishes, according to Frank, is quite important: "He actually criticizes politics from the point of view of art—a point of view happily free from the limiting conditions of all political action." Frank's chosen focus is politics, and so he does not state in his brilliant essay the necessary connection between politics and reality in general. Had he done so, his formulation might have indicated that Trilling criticizes not only politics but every aspect of human experience from the point of view of art—but that one especially notices the political consequences of such a decision because politics ordinarily involves the lives of many people. Frank goes on to cite Trilling's discovery of Hegel as authority for his point of view. The "new phenomenon of culture," in Trilling's words, had to do with "the bringing into play in the moral life of a new category of judgment, the category of quality." According to Frank, Hegel "never made the aesthetic the criterion of the moral," or of the political, but what is more important than the question of correct scholarly attribution is the principle involved. Frank locates a plausible corrective in Kant, who is said to have cautioned against "attributing the virtues of this aesthetic ideal to concrete social behavior." To do so is potentially "to endow social passivity and quietism *as such* with the halo of aesthetic transcendence." This is the heart of the matter. Though Frank had no intention of illuminating other dimensions of this issue, or of definitively penetrating the major patterns of Trilling's thought, he identified the major issue in a way we cannot afford to ignore.

Frank locates the key to Trilling's imagination in the disillusionment with politics. Trilling discovers in Hyacinth Robinson the embodiment of a heroic ideal given final shape by the character's refusal to perform the political action demanded of him. Frank's point would seem well taken. Trilling goes on to confer the "halo of aesthetic transcendence" upon Hyacinth as follows: "embodying two ideals at once[(1) the idea of revolutionary ardor, spurred by the conviction that there is human misery and that it must be addressed; (2) the ideal of civilization as a repository of beautiful things conceived by men who have learned how "to consent to the established coercive power of the world"], he takes upon himself, in full consciousness, the guilt of each. . . . By his death he instructs us in the nature of civilized life and by his consciousness he transcends it." The reader of Trilling's essay will have no trouble in consenting to his use of the word *guilt* to describe the burden taken up by Hyacinth. Clearly, there is much to be said, both for civilization and for the wish to abolish its abuses—even if the cost be great. Failure to respond to either cause will necessarily produce guilt. Allegiances ought, without question, to be divided; and yet, one wants to know whether the options need be so very divided as Trilling's argument and Hyacinth's tenuous equilibrium would have them. There are degrees in everything, of course, and one has a right to wonder about the inevitability of withdrawal and passivity as the only decent response to a guilt that no single active option promises to relieve. Frank argues that Trilling cannot but "end up in justifying a good many of the degrading objects of the social world which the will had once been required to shun and to despise"—and the point is, again, well made, as we see in its application to Hyacinth. For James's character "consents" not just to Medley and to the Venetian treasures he admires but to debased manifestations of "established coercive power." Trilling sees this and celebrates it as a heroic capitulation: "He instructs us in the nature of civilized life and by his consciousness he transcends it."

What can this mean? In what sense does one transcend a political decision and the circumstances giving rise to it? To go beyond something in a fruitful way is to move on to something better, to affirm a condition of being which is superior to the mundane options one has decided to abjure. In tragedy the hero affirms a difficult possibility that is not actually possible for most of us. He chooses in such a way that our ordinary options, our evasive stratagems, seem paltry, though relatively forgivable, by contrast. We are worthy of the lives we choose to lead: that is the best that can be said. The tragic hero is better than we are, which is to say, ill equipped to remain among us under the accepted conditions of our lives. He transcends what we take to be ordinary civilized life by challenging the primacy of our strongest commitment: to life itself, to our comfort and security, to the well-being of loved ones. By his tragic action, the hero affirms our collective limitation and our greatest virtue: we are capable of choosing a course of action, of pursuing it to its conclusion, though we know our decision must be guilty, and that from the perspective of practical experience we are committing a grave folly. Does Hyacinth Robinson affirm this virtue in the appropriate spirit of tragic determination? James, surely, does not think that he does, and Dupee is surely close to the truth when he observes that Hyacinth "seems a case merely of unrequited sensibility, of the man who is too good for this world." Like a tragic hero, Hyacinth does not belong among us, but unlike his tragic counterpart, Hyacinth does not earn the sense of difference. It is, with him, entirely a matter of sensibility, of consciousness. The tragic hero realizes his exalted fate not by virtue of sheer consciousness but by a process of active engagement that both precedes and follows upon the onset of awareness. Trilling's exaltation of Hyacinth would seem to argue that the best we may expect of a Hamlet is that he recognize the treachery of his mother and uncle and dispatch himself quickly

58

before incurring further guilt for having disturbed Ophelia and polluted the life of the court. But Hamlet would not then have done what others cannot do. He would have acted not from strength, but from timidity—or from a misguided notion of his own small obligation not to disturb the universe. Hyacinth is the victim of some such misguided notion. Though we admire his intuitive vision of irremediable conflict in experience, James does not wish us to feel that he is the best our civilization has to offer. To do so would have been to mistake the special limitations of Jamesian sensibility for the definition of human reality itself. Trilling is vulnerable to the charge that he yields to the equation.

But Trilling did not insist unremittingly on this version of the tragic. In the course of his career he came to be increasingly suspicious of the heroic mode in life and in literature. Though he remained responsive to works like *The Princess* in the terms articulated in his great essay, he knew there was something valuable in the best of us that he could not get at in the model of Hyacinth's death. The heroic mode, associated as it was for Trilling with the achievement of consciousness and with a certain power of aesthetic discrimination or negative capability, had to be looked at more scrupulously as a social phenomenon. This did not entail, for Trilling, an assault on political reality, but a response to the politics of art. In his preface to the volume *Beyond Culture* (1965), Trilling wrote:

> My sense of this difficulty leads me to approach a view which will seem disastrous to many readers and which, indeed, rather surprises me. This is the view that art does not always tell the truth or the best kind of truth . . . , that it can even generate falsehood and habituate us to it, and that, on frequent occasions, it might well be subject, in the interests of autonomy, to the scrutiny of the rational intellect.

This rational intellect, Trilling goes on to say, will be most valuable to us as it is least subject to points of view and elaborated ideas imposed by a newly accredited "adversary culture." For it is the business of our contemporary adversary culture to propose in a consistently flattering way that enlightened persons detach themselves from the matrix of ordinary middle-class experience in order to achieve an autonomous relation to truth and beauty and other comparably stirring ideas. Trilling thought this a dangerous and unrealistic proposal in the uniformity with which it had come to be made. "An adversary culture of art and thought," he argued, "when it becomes well established, shares something of the character of the larger culture to which it was—to which it still is—adversary," and finally "generates its own assumptions and preconceptions, and contrives its own sanctions to protect them." The function of rational intellect at this juncture, then, was to work against the assumptions of the now dominant adversary culture, to prevent its views from achieving automatic accreditation and thereby hardening into ideology.

It had seemed to Trilling that negative capability and the various powers associated with it by Keats and others had been ample guarantee against the abuses of intellect we had each to resist. But it had also occurred to Trilling that there was a positive value in learning to make up one's mind; even that there were positive goods involved in living in the world that had nothing to do with works of art or spacious gardens or exquisitely beautiful women. There were modest goods, small decencies, comforts one might even hesitate to call pleasures. Long before he came to write the preface to *Beyond Culture*, in other words, Trilling had come intuitively to recognize the nature of his peculiar mission. Though he wished to confer upon the ordinary and long-suffering the dignity of the tragic; though he felt there might well have been a heroic dimension in the renunciation of action and the cultivation of pure spirit (or consciousness)—he knew that he was called more especially to celebrate the conditioned life and the kind of unheroic truth it might confer. This was ultimately to be the focus of Frank's criticism: in much of Trilling's work, he says, we find ourselves "enjoined to treat the most casual conventions of the family life of the middle class as the sacrosanct conditions of life itself." For Trilling came to feel, in Frank's conclusive formulation, that his task was "to defend not freedom but the virtues of acknowledging necessity." Though I should like to omit the word *sacrosanct*, which conveys a quality I do not ordinarily find in Trilling, Frank's criticism seems to me accurate as description. And I do not think, whatever Frank's original intention, that the description speaks ill of Trilling or of the impact his work has had in the context of the present adversary culture. If the defense of freedom has become for us an inflexible ideology and if to be free means for many people to be free to do anything at all, then "the virtues of acknowledging necessity" cannot be too emphatically stressed. These virtues are not likely to be appreciated by those with an appetite for experimental life-styles, but Trilling surely had a right to expect some support from people who lived in families and could respond to the milder decencies of domestic life.

Obviously there are imaginative risks in Trilling's position, as he himself acknowledged when he warned of "a debilitation of the American psychic tone, the diminution of moral tension." The inclination to acquiesce too readily in the given state of things always threatens to produce a slackening of attention and available energy.

For the most part, I should have to say, Trilling was proof against this risk. Even when his theme is nothing but the small tribulations and successes of the domestic routine, he subtly enlarges his subject by introducing a kind of moral tension which is a function of his capacity always to generate doubt and formulate genuine questions. He seemed always a little amazed at his attraction to domestic order and the decent virtues. As a modern, he had been educated in the literature of extremity, in the spirit of apocalypse. He had every reason to be skeptical —and he remained skeptical—of the settled life, of the peaceful middle-class conception of the human. But what was he to do, he seemed to say in one work after another. One's pulses might be quickened by works of literature, by one's steady cultivation of challenging ideas, but there was a life to be lived, and actual persons with whom to deal. One did not on that account decide to leave off one's acquaintance with Mann or with Proust or with the other modernist writers who had introduced modern readers to the abyss. But one read them, somehow, differently. One pressed them a little on matters they may not have thought to address. One managed to search out their limitations, the compensatory elements in their work that bespoke an unwillingness to deal with the genuine options of the settled life. One managed, finally, to extend one's sense of the canon of the acceptable—one found a place for Orwell, for Howells; one dwelt, richly and sympathetically, on Flaubert's domestic and pecuniary relations with a niece who disappointed him; one was permitted to speak on behalf of private material interests, to praise dumb objects and the satisfaction one might take in them: "The very stupidity of things has something human about it, something meliorative, something even liberating. Together with the stupidity of the old unthinking virtues it stands against the ultimate and absolute power which the unconditioned idea can develop."[21] Is this ideological conservatism? Does it bespeak a diminution of psychic tone? I think not.

There is one work of Trilling's that—better than any other—"contains" the various elements of his thought and, instead of holding them in permanent suspension, brings them to something like a resolution. I am speaking of his story "The Other Margaret," not as famous as "Of This Time, Of That Place" but no less interesting. I cannot here devote extended attention to the story, but it is surely worth more than passing reference. Its subject is precisely the life of settled affection and mundane conflict we have been discussing. Its position—if it may be said

---

21. See the essay on Orwell in *The Opposing Self*. Trilling's most sustained theoretical consideration of these issues is in *Sincerity and Authenticity* (Cambridge, Mass.: Harvard, 1972), a volume whose expository precision is matched by a firmness of attitude not always evident elsewhere. It might be said, in fact, that *Sincerity and Authenticity* elaborates a devastating critique of "the unconditioned idea," indicating how it has achieved its present eminence in our culture and, also, the kind of thinking by which it may be resisted. That "the unconditioned idea" was of primary concern to Trilling is evidenced by the concluding chapter of his book, in which he turns his attention to several peculiar and pernicious developments in the thought of our time. He calls his chapter "The Authentic Unconscious" and speaks of the fashionable notion "that madness is health, that madness is liberation and authenticity." Trilling recommends in his final paragraph that we give "due weight to the likelihood that those who respond positively to the doctrine don't have it in mind to go mad, let alone insane"; and with this thought the reader is a little equipped to attach the requisite "conditioning" to the idea. What Trilling objects to is not so much the idea as the fact that it "is assented to so facilely, so without what used to be called seriousness." We note the confidence with which Trilling here resorts to the standard of seriousness, without compromising the ambivalence with which he customarily engages "values" earlier associated with that standard.

to have any—is politically liberal and meliorative: it recognizes that there are problems in the world, that it is useful to be aware of them, and that very few are susceptible of social or political solutions. Its technical range is, deliberately, limited: one voice, infrequent modulations of tonal intensity, no experiments with point of view. Its claim upon us is very large, and very subtle; we respond in it to a quality of authority all the more imposing for the fact that the authority has no large merit or definable conviction to uphold it.

The voice that addresses us in the story is Trilling's, and though it speaks in what the textbooks call a third-person omniscient point of view, it is determined to limit itself as much as possible to the perspective of Stephen Elwin. Elwin is, from what we can tell, a decent and sensible person. He is, moreover, deeply reflective in all of the ways we take to be characteristic of Trilling. Though he is not an international literary figure but a publisher of scientific books "in a small but successful way," Elwin commands our attention: he registers subtle shifts in conversation, and knows how to take hold of an exchange without appearing cruel or insensitive to his companions; he has an eye for works of art and is capable of extended reflection on the purpose and meaning of objects he admires; he slides—in a manner that reflects intellectual dexterity and a certain provoking glibness—from direct observation to sweeping generalization with little queasiness about the hypothetical element in his thought. He is, we may say quite bluntly, a real intellectual. Whatever the limitations we observe in his knowledge of himself or the depth of his concern for others, he has the author's confidence, and we are hard put to withhold ours. When, in a powerful sequence set on a New York West Side bus, Elwin comes face to face with the mundane cruelty common to every life, he makes so much of the reflected experience that we are moved—in gratitude—to forgive his inability to do anything but reflect.

The entire story is told in the shadow of a portrait: Roualt's king with a spray of flowers in his hand. As the story opens, Elwin stands back to admire a reproduction of the painting, which he has just bought at an art shop. Though the portrait does not remain at the center of our attention once we have passed with Elwin out of the art shop, it hovers at the margins of consciousness, waiting to be brought in, to be taken up to deliver what promises to be a decisive blow when such a blow seems required. The portrait, in Elwin's sense of it, is a veritable emblem of spiritual and worldly authority. We see in the king a range of powers we have not seen combined before in Trilling in so certain a way, and we understand what it is Trilling has wished all along to draw for us without any accompanying belief it could be convincingly done: "A person looking at it for the first time might find it repellent, even brutal or cruel." "The king, blackbearded and crowned, faced in profile to the left. He had a fierce quality that had modulated, but not softened, to authority. One could feel of him . . . that he had passed beyond ordinary matters of personality and was worthy of the crown he was wearing. Yet he was human and tragic." A little later, speaking with the proprietor about the war and about a young man in uniform who " 'did not want to miss sharing the experience of his generation,' " Elwin feels a "familiar emotion in which he could not distinguish guilt from envy." Trilling does not take the emotion very far by way of elaboration, but he knows how to shut it off for Elwin: "Now it comforted him to think that this man with the black beard and the flower had done his fighting without any remarks about experience and generations." Having passed beyond the realm of the ordinary, Roualt's king may be said to have about him a tragic quality: he doesn't mind, apparently, that he should seem "fierce" or "cruel." The implicit point is that he must necessarily seem so to those for whom the commitment to fight is itself "brutal," whatever the cause, whatever the way in which one conducts oneself. The king's "tragic" authority is, for Trilling, a function of his capacity *to be*—to know who and what he is—and, more gravely, to know what must be done as fully as he knows what is not to be done.

The title of the story refers to a black servant employed by the Elwins, a servant who happens to bear the same name as Elwin's thirteen-year-old daughter, Margaret. It is the business of the story to suggest a momentous connection between the two Margarets and to represent the process of thought wherein Elwin is reconciled to their strange 'likeness' while holding at the edge of consciousness the sobering image of Roualt's king, with all he implies. Though there is more to the story, the appropriation by consciousness of a difficult and complex truth is clearly Trilling's major concern. We see this in Trilling's tendency to play with the implications of a thought or fact before providing the thought or fact itself. Regularly the reader's attention is drawn to the sequences of intellection as well as to its object. In this sense, Elwin's daughter matters less to us as readers than the uses Elwin makes of her. There is nothing heartless in this. The reader is not made to feel that Elwin cares less for his daughter than he should. He is the sort of man, like Trilling, for whom thinking is as natural as feeling, and there is no reason given in the story why the one should obstruct the other. The reader, of course, is not required to share Elwin's depth of feeling for his daughter, only to believe that he is capable of the feeling and that she might plausibly inspire it in him. Our feelings, such as they are, hang back a little in this story. The mood is contemplative, as it is likely to be when the drama before us is primarily a drama of consciousness. The impulse is to observe, to be as discriminating as our host-narrator and his protagonist, to draw and to test conclusions. Here and there we are troubled by the sense that there may be less here than meets Elwin's—or Trilling's—eye, but we are disposed to grant every benefit of the doubt to so subtle a recorder of impressions. Though until the final pages of a long story we cannot say why Trilling has named his story for the "other Margaret," we are confident in the cogency of his purpose.

But why should Trilling have entitled his story as he did? The maid appears only briefly in her own person. She is discussed by members of Elwin's family, but she seems to be taken up in the way one discusses an issue: she is a problem, the sort of problem one must have a formulated policy to address. To be blunt, Margaret is black; she has a tendency to sullenness and insubordination; worse, her feelings of envy and resentment are generalized into an encompassing animosity—barely controlled—whose most tangible expression is the frequent breaking of valuable objects. Margaret's "hostilities" are not pretty facts, taken together, and they would seem to demand some firmness of response. There is none. Elwin knows about such responses as one knows the rites and habits of ancient peoples: one is interested in them, one tries through an effort of historical imagination to recapture some sense of what those peoples may have felt, one may even long to have lived in a time when firm counsel and strong emotions were possible. But one would be a fool to emulate what is, definitively, past, to adopt postures that are insupportable and positively anachronous in the present moment. For persons who do undertake that sort of hopeless emulation we reserve at best a species of kindly condescension, an irony whose savor is conferred by its implicit acknowledgment of "reality." It is in such a way that Elwin looks, familiarly, even tenderly, at his daughter, when she moves to enact her commitment to simple truths that no one but a child can any longer insist upon. Is it obvious that one may not say nasty things about 'unfortunate' black people, that because they are 'disadvantaged'—as the saying goes—they may not justly be held accountable for the things they do? It is young Margaret's conviction that such are indeed the 'obvious' imperatives under which civilized people must live. "In that world," Elwin reflects, "one knew where one was, one knew that to say 'things' about Jews was bad and that working men were good. And *therefore*."

Elwin can no more bring himself to say "things" than young Margaret thinks she can, but there is a point for both of them at which mind is "unable to resist a fact," at which, though incapable of doing anything much about it, Elwin brings himself beyond the obligatory liberal sentiments. The simple fact of the matter is never simple: the maid may be, as Elwin's wife puts it, " 'a thoroughly disagreeable person, a nasty, mean person.' " She is also responsible—must be responsible—for the things she does, even for the objects she deliberately breaks. But who is to hold her responsible? Who is to say that the maid must pay for the broken china? Just as the will is helpless to resist a palpable fact when it presents itself to a decent intelligence, so will is unable to mount an assault on reality itself in behalf of a scruple to which reality is generally indifferent. This is the kind of truth Trilling respects, the kind of truth which is the burden of living in a contemporary universe. The "other Margaret" is that figure of the human, all too human with which we must contend, the figure which defeats brave hopes, ideals, and extravagant sympathies. She is Trilling's emblem of the real, and before her we can have no conviction in our competence to deal with things in better than a modest—and finally unsatisfactory—way. Margaret is the world's intransigence which at once challenges and defeats consciousness: defeats it in the sense that it is made to feel more than a little unworthy of its fine powers, helpless to translate what it knows into an effectual action.

We spoke earlier of a connection between the two Margarets, and it is unmistakably a part of Trilling's intention. The daughter cannot bear to hear her parents speak ill of the servant. She is "modern"; her teacher has told her that black people cannot be blamed for what they do, that they are victims of "society"; her father, whom she loves, is himself reticent about "things," habitually keeps his critical observations to himself, and surely cannot encourage in his child a sophisticated skepticism towards the liberal pieties. Trilling is not, however, predominantly interested here in the race question or in the liberal pieties. Both are part of his larger concern with the moral life, with the way in which we come to feel a part of that life. He has Elwin put the two Margarets together because they belong together. For all their difference, they depend on one another as, at an earlier point in the story, perpetrators and victims had been placed side by side in Elwin's mind: "links in the great chain of the world's rage." The two Margarets are "links" in that sense and in others. They stand opposed, in mutual incomprehension, the one wanting to be 'good', the other to 'get even', but never really moving towards a rapprochement neither would know how to accommodate. Such a rapprochement would involve a capacity to look at one another steadily, not as types or symbols but as persons—still largely impenetrable but no less inviting for all that. Elwin thinks to bring them together by an act of imagination—not will, but imagination. He knows that they must remain apart, opposed, that his daughter is too young to see what is at stake for her in the presence of the servant; that the servant does not wish to be deprived of her anger. He cannot make them look at one another, any more than he can make himself like what he sees in the servant or approve the sentimental pieties in which his daughter has been tutored. He can, though, imagine the link between the Margarets. He can learn to see them as participating in a reality of which neither is fully conscious. He can make them more real, more present to himself, by penetrating to the living substance that makes them what they are. For it is a substance in which he participates as well. The mingled guilt and envy Elwin earlier in the story permitted himself to register in another setting is very much the substance in the context of which both Margarets must be located: in the domain of guilt and envy and also fear.

At the end of the story the servant smashes a ceramic lamb young Margaret had made and presented that day as an early birthday greeting to her mother. The child's investment in the object had been substantial, the pleasure it was to have given evident in the mother's ecstatic reception of the gift. The child can no longer control her anger; the "good sentiments" will not serve: she repeats, again and again, that the other Margaret "meant to do it." Elwin's response is so predictable as almost to be pathetic. He notices at once that the servant "looked only frightened": "For her, almost more than for his own Margaret, Elwin felt sad. He said, 'It's all right, Margaret. Don't worry, it's all right.' It was a foolish and weak thing to say. . . . But he had to say it, weak and foolish as it was." But there is more. There is the child to comfort, and both Elwin and his wife know exactly what must be said to her: "They knew that they could only offer the feeble lying of parents to a child. But they were determined to continue. 'Oh, no,' Elwin said, 'it just happened.' And he wondered if the king, within his line of vision as he stood there trying to comfort his daughter, would ever return to the old, fine, tragic power, for at the moment he seemed only quaint, extravagant and beside the point."

Trilling, then, is taking on a subject a good deal broader than the domestic habits of the urban middle class. He is not, in the conclusion to his story, limiting himself to the problems of child rearing. It is not for his daughter's sake alone that Elwin tries to comfort her by telling her at last that she did not see what she saw. Had young Margaret been an adult, Elwin would not have had to lie to her, for in his view she would then have known how to lie for herself: she would have seen what happened, registered the fact, and moved quickly to dismiss it. Earlier in the story, Elwin privately acknowledges the other Margaret's culpability, but goes on to reflect as follows: "The very costliness of the objects which proved Margaret's animosity, the very affection which the Elwins felt for them, made the whole situation impossible to consider." We turn over the recurrent sentiments in their echoing phrases: "impossible to consider," "weak and foolish"; we ponder the story's final words, so unremitting in a certain kind of uneasy candor that is less than what it takes itself to be: "quite unable, whatever he might have hoped and wanted, to give her any better help than that." Trilling's subject, after all, is nothing less than the last fact of moral life, "the insupportable fact," as he calls it. His concern is to underline, for all to see, what is left to us to do, no matter what we feel or think or will. Trilling's ultimate subject here, as it was in all his writings, is wisdom, 'the bottom line', that which each is given to know—and how we come truly to possess it.

The objects of wisdom cannot be the same for every man, but there is a wisdom Trilling feels we may well hold in common. This is a wisdom more of attitude than of position, a quality of moral tone rather than moral will. It is an attitude shaped by a constant fear—or perhaps a dread more generalized than the word *fear* can say. We find the key to this attitude in Elwin's brief reflection on his daughter's unhappiness: "But Elwin knew that it was not because the other Margaret hated her that his Margaret wept, but because she had with her own eyes seen the actual possibility of what she herself might do, the insupportable fact of her own moral life." Here at last is the connection between the Margarets that Trilling has wished to effect. And it is all but obvious that the connection, so put, implicates Elwin and the rest of us as surely as it defines the Margarets as links in the same chain. What does every man fear? In the terms of Trilling's wisdom, he fears the sight of blood on his own hands. He dreads the specter of warranted guilt, in place of which he had sooner be subject to eternal doubt and to the sense of himself as a diminished being. Better to know—early and for all time—that we are limited in crucial ways than to will a transcendence or, at least, a modest grandeur, which we cannot have and do not deserve. If guilt is to be our portion for a general failure to act, let it be a moderate guilt, diffuse and partial, rather than an awful guilt suffered on behalf of what has been done. Better to live with the might-have-been than with the certainty of difficult actions completed and, inevitably, consequential. Trilling knows that there are also consequences in the resistance to action, but these are consequences wise men will know better how to manage than others.

The "tragic power" associated in the story with Roualt's king is made in the perspective of Trilling's final wisdom to seem "quaint, extravagant and beside the point." This does not, of course, constitute a repudiation of those "tragic" figures Trilling had elsewhere been assiduous to celebrate. The dismissal of Roualt's king simply points up what we have been at intermittent pains to argue all along: that it was not "tragic power" Trilling was avid to exalt, but a certain kind of wisdom. This wisdom would necessarily take different shapes in different persons but would still be recognizable to us in its various typical manifestations. Hyacinth Robinson is wise, though he does not know how to live with his wisdom: he remains a child, we recall, in Trilling's view. Dr. Howe is wiser still, in his knowing how to live as a diminished being, fully conscious of the process by which he has been diminished. And Elwin is wisest of all, with his conflicted awareness, his ambivalent status as family man, faulty father, dubious protector, and his ability to hold in the mind the image of Roualt's king alongside the image of the needy daughter.

There is a certain discomfort we must feel, confronted with Trilling's version of wisdom, with all it says of our collective diminution and of the ironic 'knowing' gestures that are all we have in the way of legitimate response to the charge of inertia. Many of us may wish to resist Trilling, to insist that more is possible to us than he imagined, and that we need not be willfully deceived to take arms against what we feel ourselves encouraged to become. Some of us may even continue to feel that a politics is conceivable and legitimate at a time when every idea is converted to a cause and to be adversary is to be instantly authenticated even by one's ideological opponents. Trilling would not have been unhappy with our discomfort, would likely have seen in it a 'healthy' response to the cautionary perspectives of an 'elder'. If a story like "The Other Margaret" does nothing else, it must surely remind us that there are "insupportable" facts in "the moral life" and that the most insupportable of all is likely to be our own inability to be, to feel, to think what we can—even fitfully—imagine for ourselves.

In his famous essay "On The Teaching of Modern Literature,"[22] Trilling speaks of his struggle to "disguise" his own relation to modernist literature in his attempts to mediate this literature for young students who are bound to have trouble with the moral universe of Mann, of Gide, of Proust and others like them. He decides, though, not to disguise his relation to this work, "my commitment to it, my fear of it, my ambivalence toward it." For if the work was not to be 'made use of'—not to be betrayed by mere 'sentimental' or 'literary' appropriation of an idea-content all too easily domesticated by the standard 'adversary' will—it would have to be encountered with the necessary toughness and ambivalence: "These structures," Trilling argues, "were not pyramids or triumphal arches, they were manifestly contrived to be not static and commemorative but mobile and aggressive, and one does not describe a quinquereme or a howitzer or a tank without estimating how much *damage* it can do." As with the modernist masters to whom Trilling was so ambivalently attached, we cannot properly disguise our relation to Trilling himself. If we loved him, if we still find in his writings one of the consistent pleasures of literary experience, we must direct at his work that quality of aggressive engagement he honored in his own transactions with the writers he loved. Perhaps there is more of the 'triumphal arch' and of the commemorative icon in Trilling's work than he would have liked to think; and perhaps, therefore, one cannot afford to be quite so aggressive in 'attacking' his version of wisdom as he would have wished. Perhaps. What we can do, in thinking of Trilling's work, is to grant to it—in Trilling's words— "the complex fullness of its appropriate life."

22. Trilling, "On the Teaching of Modern Literature," pp. 3–30, in *Beyond Culture*.